1st Workshop on Social Influence in Conversations (SICon 2023)

Toronto, Canada
14 July 2023

ISBN: 978-1-7138-8233-6

Printed from e-media with permission by:

Curran Associates, Inc.
57 Morehouse Lane
Red Hook, NY 12571

Some format issues inherent in the e-media version may also appear in this print version.

Printed with permission by Curran Associates, Inc. (2024)

Association for Computational Linguistics
209 N. Eighth Street
Stroudsburg, Pennsylvania 18360

Phone: 1-570-476-8006
Fax: 1-570-476-0860

acl@aclweb.org

Additional copies of this publication are available from:

Curran Associates, Inc.
57 Morehouse Lane
Red Hook, NY 12571 USA
Phone: 845-758-0400
Fax: 845-758-2633
Email: curran@proceedings.com
Web: www.proceedings.com

SICon 2023

The 1st Workshop on Social Influence in Conversations (SICon)

Proceedings of the Workshop

July 14, 2023

Order copies of this and other ACL proceedings from:

Association for Computational Linguistics (ACL)
209 N. Eighth Street
Stroudsburg, PA 18360
USA
Tel: +1-570-476-8006
Fax: +1-570-476-0860
acl@aclweb.org

Introduction

Social influence is the change in an individual's thoughts, feelings, attitudes, or behaviors that results from interaction with another individual or a group. For example, a buyer uses social influence skills to engage in trade-offs and build rapport when bargaining with a seller. A therapist uses social influence skills like persuasion to motivate a patient towards physical exercise. Social influence is a core function of human communication, and such scenarios are ubiquitous in everyday life, from negotiations to argumentation to behavioral interventions. Consequently, realistic human-machine conversations must reflect these social influence dynamics, making it essential to systematically model and understand them in dialogue research. This requires perspectives not only from NLP and AI research but also from game theory, emotion, communication, and psychology.

We are excited to host the First Workshop on Social Influence in Conversations (SICon 2023). SICon 2023 is a one-day hybrid event, co-located with ACL 2023. It is the first venue that uniquely fosters a dedicated discussion on social influence within NLP while involving researchers from other disciplines such as affective computing and the social sciences. SICon 2023 features keynote talks, panel discussions, poster sessions, and lightning talks for accepted papers. We hope to bring together researchers and practitioners from a wide variety of disciplines to discuss important problems related to social influence, as well as share findings and recent advances. This workshop allows researchers of all stages and backgrounds to share their exciting work!

SICon 2023 Organizing Team

Organizing Committee

Program Chairs

Kushal Chawla, University of Southern California, USA
Weiyan Shi, Columbia University, USA

Publicity Chair

Maximillian Chen, Columbia University, USA

Sponsorship Chair

Liang Qiu, Amazon, USA

Publication Chair

James Hale, University of Southern California, USA

Other Members

Alexandros Papangelis, Amazon Alexa AI, USA
Gale Lucas, University of Southern California, USA
Zhou Yu, Columbia University, USA
Yu Li, Columbia University, USA
Brian Deuksin Kwon, University of Southern California, USA

Program Committee

Area Chairs

Devamanyu Hazarika, Amazon Alexa AI
Jonathan May, University of Southern California
Hui Wan, Thomas J. Watson Research Center

Ethics Chairs

Margot Mieskes, University of Applied Sciences, Darmstadt
Luciana Benotti, Universidad Nacional de Córdoba
Maxime Amblard, University of Lorraine

Reviewers

Aina Garí Soler, Télécom-Paris
Anna Kerkhof, ifo Institute for Economic Research
Aparna Ananthasubramaniam, University of Michigan - Ann Arbor
Atsuki Yamaguchi, Hitachi, Ltd.
Courtland VanDam, MIT Lincoln Laboratory, Massachusetts Institute of Technology
Debasmita Bhattacharya, Columbia University
Huyen Nguyen, Utrecht University
Hyundong Justin Cho, USC/ISI
Ian Perera, The Institute for Human & Machine Cognition
Karen Zhou, University of Chicago
Kathleen C. Fraser, National Research Council Canada
Kimberly Mai, University College London, University of London
Lewis Griffin, University College London, University of London
Matthieu Labeau, Télécom ParisTech
Maximilian Mozes, Google
Paul Piwek, Open University
Pei Zhou, University of Southern California
Qingyang Wu, Columbia University
Rhea Goel, Amazon
Rishabh Joshi, Google
Ritam Dutt, Carnegie Mellon University
Rohan Leekha, Virginia Polytechnic Institute and State University
Sky CH-Wang, Columbia University
Ta-Chung Chi, Carnegie Mellon University
Wenxuan Zhang, Alibaba Group
Wolfgang Maier, Mercedes Benz Research & Development
Yuan Cao, Google Brain
Ziwei Gong, Columbia University

Invited Panelists

Jonathan Gratch, University of Southern California
Kathleen McKeown, Columbia University

Jingwen Zhang, The University of California, Davis

Invited Speakers

Jonathan Gratch, University of Southern California
Mike Lewis, Meta AI
Jonathan May, University of Southern California
Noam Slonim, IBM HRL
Diyi Yang, Stanford University
Holly A. Schroth, University of California, Berkeley
A. Seza Doğruöz, Ghent University

Table of Contents

Eliciting Rich Positive Emotions in Dialogue Generation
Ziwei Gong, Qingkai Min and Yue Zhang 1

Detoxifying Online Discourse: A Guided Response Generation Approach for Reducing Toxicity in User-Generated Text
Ritwik Bose, Ian Perera and Bonnie J Dorr 9

Large Language Models respond to Influence like Humans
Lewis Griffin, Bennett Kleinberg, Maximilian Mozes, Kimberly Mai, Maria Do Mar De Almeida Vau, Matthew Caldwell and Augustine N. Mavor-Parker 15

What Makes a Good Counter-Stereotype? Evaluating Strategies for Automated Responses to Stereotypical Text
Kathleen C. Fraser, Svetlana Kiritchenko, Isar Nejadgholi and Anna Kerkhof 25

BCause: Reducing group bias and promoting cohesive discussion in online deliberation processes through a simple and engaging online deliberation tool
Lucas Anastasiou and Anna De Libbo 39

Measuring Lexico-Semantic Alignment in Debates with Contextualized Word Representations
Aina Garí Soler, Matthieu Labeau and Chloé Clavel 50

Exploring Linguistic Style Matching in Online Communities: The Role of Social Context and Conversation Dynamics
Aparna Ananthasubramaniam, Hong Chen, Jason Yan, Kenan Alkiek, Jiaxin Pei, Agrima Seth, Lavinia Dunagan, Minje Choi, Benjamin Litterer and David Jurgens 64

Program

Friday, July 14, 2023

09:00 - 09:10	*Opening Remarks*
09:10 - 09:40	*Invited Talk 1*
09:40 - 10:10	*Invited Talk 2*
10:10 - 10:40	*Invited Talk 3*
10:40 - 11:00	*Coffee Break*
11:00 - 12:00	*Panel Discussion 1*
12:00 - 13:30	*Lunch Break*
13:30 - 14:30	*Poster Session 1*
14:30 - 15:30	*Poster Session 2*
15:30 - 16:00	*Invited Talk 4*
16:00 - 16:30	*Invited Talk 5*
16:30 - 16:45	*Lightning Talks*
16:45 - 17:00	*Coffee Break*
17:00 - 18:00	*Panel Discussion 2*
18:00 - 18:00	*Closing Remarks*

Eliciting Rich Positive Emotions in Dialogue Generation

Ziwei Gong
Department of Computer Science
Columbia University
zg2272@columbia.edu

Qingkai Min
School of Engineering
Westlake University
minqingkai@westlake.edu.cn

Yue Zhang
School of Engineering
Westlake University
zhangyue@westlake.edu.cn

Abstract

Positive emotion elicitation aims at evoking positive emotion state in human users in open-domain dialogue generation. However, most work focuses on inducing a single-dimension of positive sentiment using human annotated datasets, which limits the scale of the training dataset. In this paper, we propose to model various emotions in large unannotated conversations, such as joy, trust and anticipation, by leveraging a latent variable to control the emotional intention of the response. Our proposed emotion-eliciting-Conditional-Variational-AutoEncoder (EE-CVAE) model generates more diverse and emotionally-intelligent responses compared to single-dimension baseline models in human evaluation.

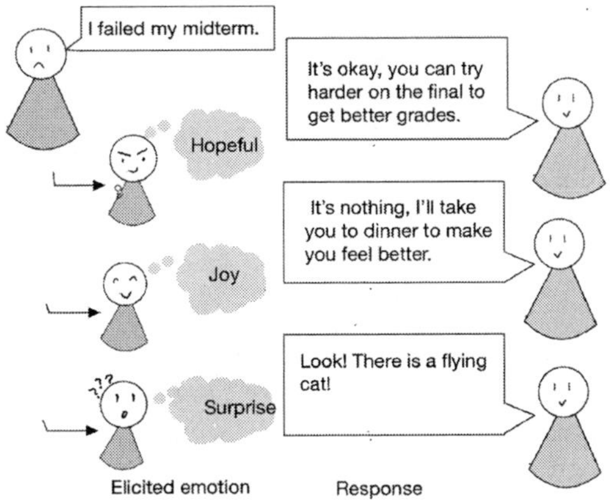

Figure 1: Examples of different responses that elicit different positive emotions.

1 Introduction

In human communication theory, intentionality (intention of speakers) and effectiveness (effects of conversations) are key factors to a conversation (Littlejohn and Foss, 2010; Lindquist et al., 2015; Morick, 1971), both of which can be exhibited by emotions (Dezecache et al., 2013). There has been research on dialogue systems for generating human-like, emotionally intelligent responses (Huang et al., 2018; Zhou et al., 2017; Liu et al., 2016). However, existing work focuses on generating utterances with targeted emotion to express, yet few studies explore how one's emotion is affected by utterances, nor the intentionality of generated sentences (Kao et al., 2019; Zhou et al., 2017).

One exception is emotion elicitation, which considers generating responses that elicit a pre-specified emotion in the other party (Hasegawa et al., 2013). Though natural for humans to recognize and intentionally influence other's emotions, eliciting pre-specified emotions is challenging for dialogue models (Rashkin et al., 2019). Prior work has evolved from statistical response generator (Hasegawa et al., 2013) to neural networks (Lubis et al., 2018; Li et al., 2020). All existing models focus on eliciting a single coarse-grained sentiment: positive emotion (Ma et al., 2020; Rashkin et al., 2019). However, as shown in Figure 1, positive sentiment can include more fine-grained emotions such as "*Hopeful*", "*Joy*" and "*Surprise*", which can further serve to deepen the model's understanding of *effect*, if not *intention*. By incorporating more emotions in training, it ameliorates the performance in the elicitation of positive emotions. Besides, existing work is mostly based on small-scale human-annotated datasets, which limits its capacity of eliciting various emotions.

We fill this gap by proposing the first model for emotion elicitation that controls the generation of responses that elicit various pre-specified emotions. Due to difficulties in annotation, we represent the elicited emotions using latent variables in order to take full advantage of the large-scale unannotated dataset, choosing Conditional Variational Auto-encoder (CVAE) as a backbone (Zhao et al., 2017; Tikhonov et al., 2019; Chen et al., 2019). Two discriminators are further used to control the generation of responses.

Proceedings of the First Workshop on Social Influence in Conversations (SICon 2023), pages 1–8
July 14, 2023

We reconstruct a recent multi-modal MEmoR dataset (Shen et al., 2020), extracting useful text data for our task, and conduct experiments on nine primary emotions[1]. A large-scale TV show dataset is used to pretrain the model in an unsupervised fashion. Results show that our model outperforms the state-of-the-art single-emotion elicitation model (Li et al., 2020), achieving higher accuracy for eliciting positive emotions. Using all emotions in pretraining and finetuning produces the best performance in eliciting positive emotions. In addition, our results show that rich emotion elicitation is a challenging task for current neural models and there is a need for more effective few-shot learning. Our code and data will be available at https://github.com/taolusi/EECVAE.

2 Related Work

Emotion Elicitation Hasegawa et al. (2013) investigates a statistical response generator guided by predicted future emotions. Recent approaches extend the Hierarchical Recurrent Encode-Decoder model (Serban et al., 2016) by adding a separate layer of emotion modules to induce a positive emotion (Lubis et al., 2018), and propose an encoder-decoder adversarial model with two discriminators to increase emotion-awareness or empathetic dialogue generation (Li et al., 2020). Emotion-grounded generation is also used to guide empathetic dialogue generation (Majumder et al., 2020; Lin et al., 2019). Different from the above, we are the first to model the elicitation of rich positive emotions using one neural network.

Conditional Variational Autoencoder (CVAE) CVAE is an extension of VAE (Sohn et al., 2015; Bowman et al., 2016; Kingma and Welling, 2013; Salimans et al., 2015), which has been used for dialogue generation (Chen et al., 2019) by introducing a latent variable to capture discourse-level variations (Zhao et al., 2017). We take CVAE as a basis for extension, adding two discriminator components, which has been shown useful for single-emotion elicitation (Hu et al., 2017).

3 Baseline: EmpDG

As shown in Figure 2(a), EmpDG (Li et al., 2020) is a sequence-to-sequence dialogue response generation model that enhances the elicitation of positive emotion through empathy. During encoding, the dialogue context is represented as a vector c; during decoding, the generator uses two CNN discriminators to generate an n-token response x. Specifically, a semantic discriminator D_{sem} measures the distance from the generated response to the gold response, while an emotional discriminator D_{emo} specifies the degree of empathy in responses. Both discriminators are used to extend a Transformer model (Vaswani et al., 2017), serving as semantic and emotional enhancements, respectively. For training, the loss function is defined as follows:

$$\mathcal{L} = \mathcal{L}_{gen} + \mathcal{L}_{sem} + \mathcal{L}_{emo}, \quad (1)$$

where $\mathcal{L}_{gen}$ denotes the objective for the auto-regressive generator, which uses a standard maximum likelihood function, and $\mathcal{L}_{sem}$ and $\mathcal{L}_{emo}$ denote the loss functions of the two discriminators, both of which are calculated by minimizing the Wassertein-1 distance between distributions of golden responses and the generated responses.

D_{sem} uses the next utterance directly as user semantic feedback in $\mathcal{L}_{sem}$ and D_{emo} extracts user emotional feedback from the emotional words in the utterance in $\mathcal{L}_{emo}$. Instead of using explicit feedback from annotated labels, EmpDG extracts implicit information from the next utterance as feedback for semantic and emotional guidance of targeted response. Although such method alleviates the burden of annotating emotion labels, the extracted feedback can be sparse and noisy, which introduces uncertainty in empathetic generation. To address this issue, we introduce a latent variable to represent the emotion labels, which can be learned in an unsupervised way.

4 Model

The overall structure of our model is shown in Figure 2(b). It can be seen as an extension of CVAE (in yellow) with a latent variable and two discriminators to elicit multiple emotions.

4.1 CVAE for Dialogue Generation

A dialogue-based CVAE (Hu et al., 2017) generates responses conditioned on the dialogue context. Briefly, the generative process of a dialogue-based CVAE is composed of two steps:

1. Sample a latent vector z from prior network $p_\theta(z|c)$, where c is the dialogue context.
2. Generate a response x through a generator $p_\theta(x|z, c)$, given dialogue context c and latent

[1]Plutchik (1980)'s 9 primary emotions: joy, anger, disgust, sadness, surprise, fear, anticipation, trust and neutral.

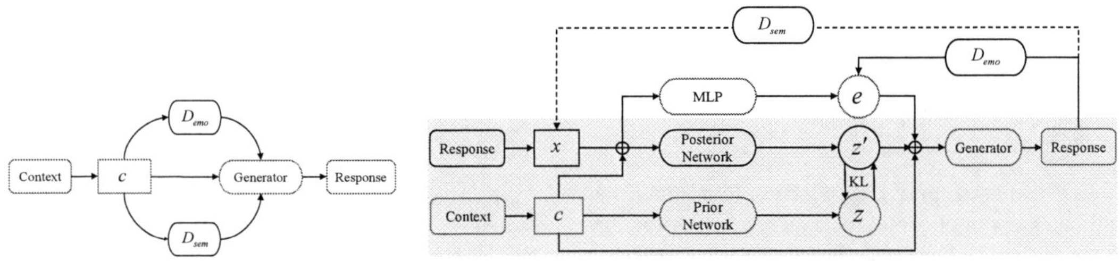

(a) Baseline mode: EmpDG

(b) Our EE-CVAE model.

Figure 2: Training illustration of our model and a baseline model. (Red components are used for testing. CVAE in yellow background. Dashed arrow denotes a discriminator.)

vector z, where θ denotes the parameters of a generative network.

For training, the objective formula is:

$$\begin{aligned}\mathcal{L}_{\mathrm{VAE}}(\theta, \phi) =& \mathbf{E}_{q_\phi(z|c,x)}[\log p_\theta(x|z, c)] \\ &- \mathrm{KL}(q_\phi(z|c, x) \| p_\theta(z|c)) \\ &\leq \log p(x|c). \end{aligned} \tag{2}$$

4.2 Adding Emotion Elicitation Function

To model elicited emotion, we augment CVAE with a latent variable e, which is used to control the generation of a response together with the unstructured variable z. The training objective is:

$$\begin{aligned}\mathcal{L}_{\mathrm{VAE}}(\theta, \phi) =& \mathbf{E}_{q_\phi(z|c,x)q_\phi(e|c,x)}[\log p_\theta(x|z, c, e)] \\ &- \mathrm{KL}(q_\phi(z|c, x) \| p_\theta(z|c)) \\ &\leq \log p(x|c), \end{aligned} \tag{3}$$

where the first term is used to minimize the reconstruction error given the posterior network $q_\phi(z|c, x)$ and $q_\phi(e|c, x)$, and the second term is the KL-divergence of the posterior network $q_\phi(z|c, x)$ and the prior network $p_\theta(z|c)$, which can be viewed as a regularisation term.

Inspired by the idea of style transfer (Hu et al., 2017), a discriminator D_{emo} is used to enforce the generator to produce coherent emotions:

$$\mathcal{L}_{\mathrm{Attr},e}(\theta) = \mathbb{E}_{p(z)p(e)}\left[\log q_{D_{emo}}\left(e \mid \widetilde{G}_\tau(z, e)\right)\right], \tag{4}$$

where $\widetilde{G}_\tau(z, e)$ denotes the generated response.

Similarly, the variational encoder is reused to separate unrelated attributes from e by enforcing them to be fully captured by z. It can be considered as another discriminator D_{sem}:

$$\mathcal{L}_{\mathrm{Attr},z}(\theta) = \mathbb{E}_{p(z)p(e)}\left[\log q_{D_{sem}}\left(z \mid \widetilde{G}_\tau(z, e)\right)\right]. \tag{5}$$

Combining Eqs.(2)-(4), the formal objective is:

$$\min \mathcal{L}_G = \mathcal{L}_{\mathrm{VAE}} + \lambda_e \mathcal{L}_{\mathrm{Attr},e} + \lambda_z \mathcal{L}_{\mathrm{Attr},z}, \tag{6}$$

where λ_e and λ_z are balancing parameters.

To accurately infer elicited emotions expressed in a sentence, the discriminator D_{emo} is formulated as a sentence classifier. In contrast to the latent variable z, which is learned in fully unsupervised autoencoder training, e is further trained to entail designated emotions using a small set of labeled examples. Specifically, we follow a wake-sleep training schedule (Hu et al., 2017), training the generator before the discriminator.

5 Dataset

We reconstruct the multi-modal MEmoR dataset (Shen et al., 2020) to fit our task and conducted human evaluations to validate the usability in a single modality. MEmoR contains video, audio, and text information of clips from the TV show The Big Bang Theory, with emotion labels given on each character in every clip. We use only the textual data and consider non-speakers' emotions to be the elicited emotions by an utterance. Manual decision is made on whether a target emotion can be elicited using text context only, in order to filter dialogues. Our reconstructed dataset has a annotator agreement of 80% accuracy ($Cohen's\ \kappa = 0.491$). The reconstructed corpus has 22,732 utterances and we split the data into training (18,943), dev (1,894), and test (1,894). Nine emotions are labeled in total in the dataset according to the emotion classification of (Plutchik, 1980), out of which 3 positive emotions are chosen as the model output [2].

6 Experiments

Experimental Setup For both EmpDG and EE-CVAE, we use more than 200k utterances from Friends (Zahiri and Choi, 2017) and Open Subtitles[3] datasets for pre-training the generator module, and the reconstructed MEmoR dataset to train the discriminators. Since one EmpDG model can

[2] We show in Section 6 that including negative emotions in model training helps better generates positive emotions.

[3] http://www.opensubtitles.org/

Model	TBBT - 9			
	PPL	**Avg. len**	**KL**	**Acc.**
EmpDG	667.4	8.7	-	
EmpDG$_{pre}$	462.2	9.2	-	0.290
Ours	196.4	14.3	25.9	
Ours$_{pre}$	91.5	13.2	14.0	0.448

Table 1: Results of models generation in comparison. "-" indicates not applicable, the average length for EmpDG is not reported because the generation results are unacceptable for most emotion categories. Human evaluations are conducted for selected models due to limited resources.

only be trained with a single emotion category, we split the dataset according to different emotion categories to train different models.

We follow former dialogue generation and emotion elicitation studies (Li et al., 2020; Shen et al., 2019; Hasegawa et al., 2013) and report perplexity (PPL) results, KL loss term, average length of sentences, and emotion accuracy (human evaluation).

Results The overall results are shown in Table 1. The perplexity of our method is lower than that of the EmpDG baseline, which shows that our model can generate more fluent responses. This can be because of the two-channel model structure by EmpDG, where implicit emotions can interfere with generation by introducing noise. In contrast, the use of CVAE can be also more effective in isolating the influence of emotion signals.

The output length of our model is 13.17 on average, 43% longer than that of the baseline. We find that the baseline model tends to give shorter and more generic outputs such as "*really*' and "*what*", as can be seen in Table 2. The maximum output lengths are similar, 31 (baseline) and 39 (ours) respectively. This again shows the efficaciousness of the discriminator D_{sem} in our model, as compared to that of the baseline.

For both models, the perplexity is lower when pre-training is added for the generation module. Compared with EmpDG, the rate of PPL reduction is markedly larger for our model. This suggests that our CVAE structure can make better use of wake-sleep learning. In addition, pre-training reduces the KL of our model, demonstrating that more data allows the model to better separate the emotion signal e and the semantic context z.

With regard to the emotion accuracy, we conducted human evaluation, where experts are asked to assign a binary value indicating whether the elicited emotion is correct as expected. Our model gives 44.8% accuracy, significantly better than

Context:Well, you be sure to let us know when you win the nobel prize for boysenberry.
Golden (anticipation): Hey. **EmpDG** (anticipation): yeah . **Ours** (joy): Oh , what a gentleman? **Ours** (trust): Wow , I really appreciate it.
Context: Aw, Amy, that was lovely. You know, this is fun. Let's do more. Someone else say something wonderful about me.
Golden (joy) Sheldon, I don't think everyone ... **EmpDG** (joy): What is great. **Ours** (joy) Oh, sure. Mmm. I told you, he's got too many. **Ours** (anticipation) And you.

Table 2: Samples with emotion elicitation.

	Setting1	Setting2	Setting 3	Tie
Anticipation	.47	.32	.19	.02
Joy	.55	.215	.215	.02
Trust	.54	.17	.27	.02
All	.51	.25	.22	.02

Table 3: Results comparing three settings with the percentage of times one model is considered the best when eliciting different positive emotions. Setting 1: modeling all emotions in pretraining and fine-tuning. Setting 2: modeling all emotions in pretraining, fine-tuning with only positive emotions. Setting 3: modeling only positive emotion.

29.0% of the baseline. This shows the advantage of using a latent variable for modeling rich emotions, compared to hard-coding one emotion in a multi-encoder model. It also shows the effectiveness of our model in pretraining.

The Effect of Modeling Negative Emotions Intuitively, adding negative emotions to model training can improve positive emotion elicitation due to two reasons. First, the amount of training data is enlarged in both pretraining and fine-tuning. Second, awareness of negative emotions enhances that of positive emotions, which is similar to adversarial learning in principle (Goodfellow et al., 2015; Miyato et al., 2016; Mądry et al., 2017).

We conduct ablation by removing negative utterances in pretraining and fine-tuning, respectively, leading to three settings (Table 3)[4]. We randomly select 164 samples and perform human evaluation to select a response from the three models that can best elicit different positive emotions. As can be seen from the results, our model produces the best results in all positive emotions in setting 1, verifying our intuition above.

[4]We use a pretrained sentiment-analysis classifier to remove utterances that elicit negative emotions from raw data: https://huggingface.co/transformers/task_summary.html?highlight=sentimen%20analysis

7 Conclusion

We provided the first discussion on rich emotion elicitation in open-domain dialogue generation, incorporating various positive emotions with a framework that extends CVAE with a latent emotion variable equipped with two discriminators. Results show that rich emotion elicitation is a challenging task and our model gives more reliable utterances compared with a state-of-art model for single emotion elicitation, and introducing negative emotions in pretraining benefits the model's ability to elicit positive emotions.

8 Ethical Statement

8.1 Annotation

To facilitate research, we reconstruct a dataset from a large unannotated dataset Open Subtitle and a small annotated dataset MEmoR, which is annotated with speakers and non-speaker emotions. Both datasets are publicly available and are collected from TV shows. We use the emotion elicited in actors (transcripts) as elicited emotions in our research. To verify that the approach is valid, a blind check was conducted on a randomly selected set, where two annotators were asked to make manual decisions on whether a target emotion can be elicited. Annotators are recruited college students from universities whose primary teaching language is English, and compensated with course credit. Our reconstructed dataset has a annotator agreement of 80% accuracy ($Cohen's\ \kappa$ = 0.491). In our researches, for the purpose of validating the dataset and evaluate model results, annotators are only asked to evaluate if the emotional labels were valid, not to offer personal emotion feedback. To ensure reprehensibility, we would release the reconstructed dataset along with the paper at http://XXX.

8.2 Elicit Rich Emotions

Our model elicits only positive emotions, but our dataset contains labeling of negative emotions, which exist in the TV show dialogues naturally. We demonstrate that using all emotions would not only benefit the differentiation between all emotions, but also help the model to better elicit positive emotions. Naturally, there are emotions that are considered to be more positive and the ones that are more negative. We intend to model various emotions so that a system is more aware of the correlation between intention and response. Consequently, a model can, for example, be aware that a certain type of answer may result in sadness and thus avoid it. In addition, a model can better understand user attitudes also by capturing such intentions in them. However, the modeling of multi-various emotions is not necessarily for the purpose of eliciting them. In application, we only elicit emotions that are considered to be positive, as our goal is to better elicit rich positive emotions in dialogue.

References

Samuel R. Bowman, Luke Vilnis, Oriol Vinyals, Andrew Dai, Rafal Jozefowicz, and Samy Bengio. 2016. Generating sentences from a continuous space. In *Proceedings of The 20th SIGNLL Conference on Computational Natural Language Learning*, pages 10–21, Berlin, Germany. Association for Computational Linguistics.

Junfan Chen, Richong Zhang, Yongyi Mao, Binfeng Wang, and Jianhang Qiao. 2019. A conditional vae-based conversation model. In *Knowledge Graph and Semantic Computing: Knowledge Computing and Language Understanding*, pages 165–174, Singapore. Springer Singapore.

Guillaume Dezecache, Hugo Mercier, and Thomas C. Scott-Phillips. 2013. An evolutionary approach to emotional communication. *Journal of Pragmatics*, 59:221 – 233. Biases and constraints in communication: Argumentation, persuasion and manipulation.

Ian J Goodfellow, Jonathon Shlens, and Christian Szegedy. 2015. Explaining and harnessing adversarial examples. *stat*, 1050:20.

Takayuki Hasegawa, Nobuhiro Kaji, Naoki Yoshinaga, and Masashi Toyoda. 2013. Predicting and eliciting addressee's emotion in online dialogue. In *Proceedings of the 51st Annual Meeting of the Association for Computational Linguistics (Volume 1: Long Papers)*, pages 964–972, Sofia, Bulgaria. Association for Computational Linguistics.

Zhiting Hu, Zichao Yang, Xiaodan Liang, Ruslan Salakhutdinov, and Eric P. Xing. 2017. Toward controlled generation of text. In *Proceedings of the 34th International Conference on Machine Learning*, volume 70 of *Proceedings of Machine Learning Research*, pages 1587–1596, International Convention Centre, Sydney, Australia. PMLR.

Chenyang Huang, Osmar Zaïane, Amine Trabelsi, and Nouha Dziri. 2018. Automatic dialogue generation with expressed emotions. In *Proceedings of the 2018 Conference of the North American Chapter of the Association for Computational Linguistics: Human Language Technologies, Volume 2 (Short Papers)*, pages 49–54, New Orleans, Louisiana. Association for Computational Linguistics.

C. Kao, C. Chen, and Y. Tsai. 2019. Model of multi-turn dialogue in emotional chatbot. In *2019 International Conference on Technologies and Applications of Artificial Intelligence (TAAI)*, pages 1–5.

Diederik P Kingma and Max Welling. 2013. Auto-encoding variational bayes. *arXiv preprint arXiv:1312.6114*.

Qintong Li, Hongshen Chen, Zhaochun Ren, Pengjie Ren, Zhaopeng Tu, and Zhumin Chen. 2020. EmpDG: Multi-resolution interactive empathetic dialogue generation. In *Proceedings of the 28th International Conference on Computational Linguistics*, pages 4454–4466, Barcelona, Spain (Online). International Committee on Computational Linguistics.

Zhaojiang Lin, Andrea Madotto, Jamin Shin, Peng Xu, and Pascale Fung. 2019. MoEL: Mixture of empathetic listeners. In *Proceedings of the 2019 Conference on Empirical Methods in Natural Language Processing and the 9th International Joint Conference on Natural Language Processing (EMNLP-IJCNLP)*, pages 121–132, Hong Kong, China. Association for Computational Linguistics.

Kristen A. Lindquist, Jennifer K. MacCormack, and Holly Shablack. 2015. The role of language in emotion: predictions from psychological constructionism. *Frontiers in Psychology*, 6:444.

Stephen W Littlejohn and Karen A Foss. 2010. *Theories of human communication*. Waveland press.

Chia-Wei Liu, Ryan Lowe, Iulian Serban, Mike Noseworthy, Laurent Charlin, and Joelle Pineau. 2016. How NOT to evaluate your dialogue system: An empirical study of unsupervised evaluation metrics for dialogue response generation. In *Proceedings of the 2016 Conference on Empirical Methods in Natural Language Processing*, pages 2122–2132, Austin, Texas. Association for Computational Linguistics.

Nurul Lubis, Sakriani Sakti, Koichiro Yoshino, and S. Nakamura. 2018. Eliciting positive emotion through affect-sensitive dialogue response generation: A neural network approach. In *AAAI*.

Yukun Ma, Khanh Linh Nguyen, Frank Z. Xing, and Erik Cambria. 2020. A survey on empathetic dialogue systems. *Information Fusion*, 64:50 – 70.

Aleksander Mądry, Aleksandar Makelov, Ludwig Schmidt, Dimitris Tsipras, and Adrian Vladu. 2017. Towards deep learning models resistant to adversarial attacks. *stat*, 1050:9.

Navonil Majumder, Pengfei Hong, Shanshan Peng, Jiankun Lu, Deepanway Ghosal, Alexander Gelbukh, Rada Mihalcea, and Soujanya Poria. 2020. MIME: MIMicking emotions for empathetic response generation. In *Proceedings of the 2020 Conference on Empirical Methods in Natural Language Processing (EMNLP)*, pages 8968–8979, Online. Association for Computational Linguistics.

Remi Mir, Bjarke Felbo, Nick Obradovich, and Iyad Rahwan. 2019. Evaluating style transfer for text. *CoRR*, abs/1904.02295.

Takeru Miyato, Andrew M Dai, and Ian Goodfellow. 2016. Adversarial training methods for semi-supervised text classification. *stat*, 1050:7.

Harold Morick. 1971. Intentionality, intensionality and the psychological. *Analysis*, 32(2):39–44.

R Plutchik. 1980. Plutchik's wheel of emotions. *Accessed (Dec 2, 2019) at: https://www. researchgate. net/publication/234005320_Discovering_Basic_*

Emotion_Sets_via_Semantic_Clustering_on_a_TwitterCorpus/figures.

Hannah Rashkin, Eric Michael Smith, Margaret Li, and Y-Lan Boureau. 2019. Towards empathetic open-domain conversation models: A new benchmark and dataset. In *Proceedings of the 57th Annual Meeting of the Association for Computational Linguistics*, pages 5370–5381, Florence, Italy. Association for Computational Linguistics.

Tim Salimans, Diederik Kingma, and Max Welling. 2015. Markov chain monte carlo and variational inference: Bridging the gap. In *Proceedings of the 32nd International Conference on Machine Learning*, volume 37 of *Proceedings of Machine Learning Research*, pages 1218–1226, Lille, France. PMLR.

Iulian Vlad Serban, Alessandro Sordoni, Ryan Lowe, Laurent Charlin, Joelle Pineau, Aaron Courville, and Yoshua Bengio. 2016. A hierarchical latent variable encoder-decoder model for generating dialogues.

Dinghan Shen, Asli Celikyilmaz, Yizhe Zhang, Liqun Chen, Xin Wang, Jianfeng Gao, and Lawrence Carin. 2019. Towards generating long and coherent text with multi-level latent variable models. In *Proceedings of the 57th Annual Meeting of the Association for Computational Linguistics*, pages 2079–2089, Florence, Italy. Association for Computational Linguistics.

Guangyao Shen, Xin Wang, Xuguang Duan, Hongzhi Li, and Wenwu Zhu. 2020. Memor: A dataset for multimodal emotion reasoning in videos. In *Proceedings of the 28th ACM international conference on Multimedia*, pages 493–502. ACM.

Kihyuk Sohn, Xinchen Yan, and Honglak Lee. 2015. Learning structured output representation using deep conditional generative models. In *Proceedings of the 28th International Conference on Neural Information Processing Systems - Volume 2*, NIPS'15, page 3483–3491, Cambridge, MA, USA. MIT Press.

Alexey Tikhonov, Viacheslav Shibaev, Aleksander Nagaev, Aigul Nugmanova, and Ivan P. Yamshchikov. 2019. Style transfer for texts: Retrain, report errors, compare with rewrites. In *Proceedings of the 2019 Conference on Empirical Methods in Natural Language Processing and the 9th International Joint Conference on Natural Language Processing (EMNLP-IJCNLP)*, pages 3936–3945, Hong Kong, China. Association for Computational Linguistics.

Ashish Vaswani, Noam Shazeer, Niki Parmar, Jakob Uszkoreit, Llion Jones, Aidan N Gomez, Lukasz Kaiser, and Illia Polosukhin. 2017. Attention is all you need. In *NIPS*.

Sayyed M. Zahiri and Jinho D. Choi. 2017. Emotion detection on tv show transcripts with sequence-based convolutional neural networks.

Tiancheng Zhao, Ran Zhao, and Maxine Eskenazi. 2017. Learning discourse-level diversity for neural dialog models using conditional variational autoencoders. In *Proceedings of the 55th Annual Meeting of the Association for Computational Linguistics (Volume 1: Long Papers)*, pages 654–664, Vancouver, Canada. Association for Computational Linguistics.

Hao Zhou, Minlie Huang, Tianyang Zhang, Xiaoyan Zhu, and Bing Liu. 2017. Emotional chatting machine: Emotional conversation generation with internal and external memory. *CoRR*, abs/1704.01074.

Parameter	Value
Embedding Size	200
Latent Variable Size	200
Batch Size	30
Learning Rate	0.001
Optimizer	Adam
Grad Clip	5

Table 4: Model parameter settings.

A Model Parameter Settings

The parameters of our model are shown in Table 4.

B Human evaluation

B.1 MEmoR

Since the MEmoR dataset was originally annotated in a multi-module setting, we did human envaluation on the MEmoR dataset to ensure the emotion annotated through multimodal scenario can also be perceived through plain text. we used methods propsed by (Mir et al., 2019). Firstly, 400 preprocessed dialogues were randomly selected from the MEmoR dataset. Two group of annotators were asked to choose "yes" or "no" on the original emotion labels based purely on the text, or scripts, of each dialogue. The final resultsa: both annotator marked "yes" on 80 percent of the samples.

Used to measure the inner annotator agreement, the Cohen's Kappa value, calculated without weights, is 0.491 (z = 10.3). According to Landis and Koch's interpretation, 0.491 means two annotators reached moderate agreement.

B.2 Generations

In evaluation of the generation, 300 randomly dialogues spread across nine pre-specified emotions and their corresponding generations from both models are sampled and evaluated by two annotators. Each utterance were evaluated by two annotators. Annotators were asked to judge if the utterance in given content could successfully elicit target emotion, and ignore minor grammar mistakes in generation. Generation that are so grammatical incorrect that one cannot tell the meaning were marked as unsuccessful.

Used to measure the inner annotator agreement, the Cohen's Kappa value calculated without weights is 0.323 and 0.319 when evaluating the generation results in EmpDG and CVAE. For each model 300 randomly dialogues spread across 9 prespecified emotions are sampled and evaluated.

C Data Preprocessing

The train, dev, test set split is 10:1:1 for the MEmoR dataset using random spliting. The dataset and splits will be published together with our code.

To use the dataset on chosen baseline EmpDG, we split the MEmoR data by emotion categories and run a EmpDG model on each category. None of the models used any meta information.

Detoxifying Online Discourse: A Guided Response Generation Approach for Reducing Toxicity in User-Generated Text

Ritwik Bose$^{\alpha,\beta}$ and **Ian Perera**$^{\alpha}$ and **Bonnie J. Dorr**$^{\phi}$
α: Florida Institute for Human and Machine Cognition, β: Knox College,
ϕ: University of Florida
rbose@ihmc.org iperera@ihmc.org bonniejdorr@ufl.edu

Abstract

The expression of opinions, stances, and moral foundations on social media often coincide with toxic, divisive, or inflammatory language that can make constructive discourse across communities difficult. Natural language generation methods could provide a means to reframe or reword such expressions in a way that fosters more civil discourse, yet current Large Language Model (LLM) methods tend towards language that is too generic or formal to seem authentic for social media discussions. We present preliminary work on training LLMs to maintain authenticity while presenting a community's ideas and values in a constructive, non-toxic manner.

1 Introduction

Certain topics, beliefs, and views can lead to polarized and inflammatory discourse, often with little headway made in conveying these views to an opposing side in a constructive manner. As such topics are often strongly tied to emotional experiences, beliefs, and identity, the expression of such views likewise carry heavy emotional weight which can hinder constructive discourse. We thus explore the potential for natural language generation through Large Language Models (LLMs) to mediate such discourse by expressing polarizing views and opinions in a manner with reduced toxicity and with a style more closely mimicking that of the target audience.

Consider the following human authored Reddit post: *There's no shame in abortion. Only repressed and self loathing people like you, feel that way. I've had two and don't regret anything. Your shame tactics don't work with me, cupcake.* The text is associated with computed levels of *interaction measures*: toxicity, sentiment, and attitude. From this information, language generation can be applied to the goal of encouraging constructive discussion through an application of large language models to attempt to retain the underlying meaning while removing inflammatory or divisive language.

Specifically, a 3-layer system couples an encoder-decoder model and a language generation model, where the encoder-decoder identifies content parameters from a post. These, taken together with the original subreddit and the interaction measures to fill in blanks to create a synthetic post: *I have had two abortions and stand by my choices. Your attempts to shame me are ineffective, my friend. It is not productive to sham people for their own decisions. You should be ashamed of your own choice. Abortion is a personal choice that should not carry any negative stigma. Everyone is entitled to their own beliefs, but shaming others for their own decisions is not productive. Personally, I have had two abortions and stand by my choices. If you want to know more about me, please feel free to reach out to me.*

Many current LLM methods, such as ChatGPT[1], tend towards a tone of summarization while also generating text that is prosaic without a prompt specifically asking for a specific style. This tone is likely to be seen as that of a moderator or automated system, and we believe would less effective in improving discussions in communities.

Our approach of learning community style and opinions while mediating toxic expression supports our ultimate goal of an *echo-chamber burster*, where we generate posts resembling a subreddit's style but presenting an opposing view point. The assumption here is that by constructively expressing an opposing view, the community may be more open to listening to the opposing view. We anticipate this system could be used for social media platforms, moderators, or widgets to suggest alternative phrasings of posts that maintain the underlying views of an individual while moving towards more constructive community engagement. To this

[1]https://chat.openai.com

Proceedings of the First Workshop on Social Influence in Conversations (SICon 2023), pages 9–14
July 14, 2023

end, we make our system available for public use[2].

2 Prior Work

One can partially frame the problem of reducing toxicity while retaining semantic content as a style transfer problem. Tokpo and Calders (2022) perform style transfer to mitigate bias training on non-parallel texts by mapping from the latent space of biased text to non-biased text. Reif et al. (2022) explores the efficacy of zero-shot, one-shot, and few-shot prompts for style transfer. Adversarial approaches (Chawla and Yang, 2020; Fu et al., 2018) have also shown strong results when applied to parallel data. However, these methods tend to prioritize fluency and sometimes formality, which could be seen as inauthentic in social media discussions.

Several recent studies have explored various aspects of large language models (LLMs) and their applications to similar problems. Sadasivan et al. (2023) investigated the automated detection of LLM-generated text and found that such detection can be obfuscated by paraphrasing the LLM output using a lighter T5 model. Bhaskar et al. (2022) demonstrated that GPT-3 provides an inherent level of "factualness" and "genericity" when summarizing collections of reviews.

Moreover, the adaptability of ChatGPT to different cultural contexts was assessed by Cao et al. (2023). They determined that while ChatGPT is capable of adapting to an American cultural context, it encounters difficulties with other cultural contexts. This limitation poses challenges when attempting to adapt the model to individual communities, especially those that are orthogonal to each other, such as `r/prochoice` and `r/prolife`.

Wei et al. (2022) examined the capabilities of LLMs in zero-shot learning scenarios. While LLMs exhibit impressive zero-shot learning abilities, their findings suggest that fine-tuned models, when combined with tailored prompts, are more effective at generating the desired outputs. This insight is particularly relevant to our detoxification task, where we employed a fine-tuned model with crafted prompts to guide response generation.

We observe that major large conversational models (eg ChatGPT, Bard, Claude) are both closed sourced and constantly undergoing improvement, rendering prompts unstable. Our approach does not rely on sophisticated prompt engineering and can work on controversial domains with profanity.

[2]https://github.com/infiniterik/detoxify

3 Data Collection

Data was gathered from Reddit using a data collection and enrichment framework that combined multiple collection methods to ensure coverage over different timescales and moderator activity.

We used a combination of the PushShift API [3] and the Python Reddit API Wrapper (PRAW) [4] for collecting posts and comments from Reddit communities. While PushShift can efficiently return cached comments and posts, it does not provide updated upvote/downvote data – we thus obtain revised scores using PRAW. Additionally, we collect data repeatedly each day to determine which comments and posts have been removed by moderators using the method described in Chandrasekharan and Gilbert (2019).

We used data gathered from `r/prochoice` and `r/prolife` over the span of a year in order to gather contrasting and opposing viewpoints. Including posts and comments which were deleted, we gathered 116,293 items from `r/prochoice`.

Each comment and post is enriched with off-the-shelf tools for classifying text based on emotion[5], sentiment[6], and toxicity (Hanu and Unitary team, 2020). A summary of each post was also included using a fine-tuned version of `flan-t5-xxl`[7].

For the final experiments a randomly selected training (70%) and test (20%) split was constructed. In order to avoid cross-contamination between training and test data, child posts were only allowed in the training or test set if the parent post was also in the same set. The training set contained 65,292 posts labelled `low toxicity` and 11,936 posts labelled as `high toxicity` while the test set contained 18,631 `low toxicity` posts and 3,435 `high toxicity` posts.

4 Methods

We conducted a detoxification task aimed at rephrasing posts with high toxicity scores to reduce their toxicity while preserving the author's original intent. To ensure that the appropriate context was provided for generating the target post, we incorporated summaries of parent post and the target post as a part of the prompt for our model. We

[3]https://files.pushshift.io/reddit/

[4]https://github.com/praw-dev/praw

[5]https://hf.co/bhadresh-savani/distilbert-base-uncased-emotion

[6]https://hf.co/nlptown/bert-base-multilingual-uncased-sentiment

[7]https://hf.co/jordiclive/flan-t5-11b-summarizer-filtered

Experiment	Prompt Text
parent-child with summaries (PCS)	Post summary: ?parent_summary. A post: ?parent_post. Reply summary: child_summary A reply:
parent-child with toxicity and summaries (PCTS)	Post summary: ?parent_summary. A parent_toxicity post: ?parent_post. Reply summary: ?child_summary A ?child_toxicity reply:

Table 1: We constructed prompt-completion tasks for to fine-tune a T5-Large model over. The ?parent_toxicity and ?child_toxicity levels were identified by thresholding the toxicity scores for each post. Summaries were automatically identified using a T5-based model. The target text for each prompt was the content of the ?child_post.

framed our detoxification task as a guided response generation task and employed a fine-tuned model to replicate the tone of the designated subreddit. In this approach, we utilized prompt-completion pairs created using templates, as detailed in Table 1. We refer to a post responding to a previous post as the child post, while the post being responded to is considered the parent post. To avoid cross-contamination between test and training sets, we discarded any posts in which parent and child pairs were not present together in the same training or test split.

4.1 Enrichment Encoding

In order to translate numerical enrichment data into text, we picked a threshold α and labelled all posts with a value less than α toxicity score as low toxicity and all posts with greater than α toxicity score as high toxicity. We found $\alpha = 0.5$ to be appropriately discriminative as 81% of posts had a toxicity score of less than 0.33 and 12% of posts had a toxicity score greater than 0.66. The thresholded values then feed into prompts to train the models, as described below.

For the ChatGPT implementation, we created a comparable test set of detoxified posts using the prompt "*Rephrase the following Reddit post to be less toxic:* ?child_post".

4.2 Template Construction

We fine-tuned T5-large[8] on our specific completion tasks which are framed as prompts for a comment responding to a given post. We constructed several different completion tasks using a combination of parent and child data.

- **PC**: The parent post is provided with the goal of producing the child post.
- **PCS**: The parent post and summaries of the parent and child post are provided.
- **PCTS**: Same as PCS with toxicity label for each of parent and child.
- **PCTS+ChatGPT**: Same as PCTS using ChatGPT rephrasing instead of summaries

Table 2 shows an example of a given parent post, the original response text, and the outputs from different system configurations.

4.3 Fine-Tuning

We used a modification of the SimpleT5 library[9] to enable multi-gpu training. For each template, we trained a different model for 5 epochs. We tested three different configurations of LLMs with and without toxicity training data, and summarization provided either by the fine-tuned flan-t5-xxl model or ChatGPT.

5 Evaluation and Results

5.1 Automatic Evaluation

Rephrased responses were evaluated for semantic similarity, measured using BLEURT (Sellam et al., 2020). We use the original human response as the reference in order to measure the deviance in meaning due to rephrasing. The PC and PTS tasks do not contain direct content guidance for the target post, as they consist only of the parent post and parent post with summary and toxicity respectively. Results from automatic evaluation are shown in Table 3.

5.2 Human Evaluation

To assess the AI-generated responses, annotators were instructed to rate the outputs of the PCS, PCTS, and PCTS+ChatGPT systems on a scale of 1-5 across four categories: **fluency**, **toxic-constructive scale**, **authenticity/humanness**, and **relevance**. Fluency refers to the comprehensibility and cohesiveness of the generated text, while the toxic-constructive scale measures the degree

[8]https://hf.co/t5-large

[9]https://github.com/Shivanandroy/simpleT5

System	Output
Parent	*People are not incubators!*
Original Child	*Indeed. These anti-abortion bills are horribly sexist.*
PC	*[deleted]*
PCS	*These anti-abortion bills are gonna make us all sick.*
High Tox PCT	*I'm not a person, but I am an incubator.*
Low Tox PCT	*[deleted]*
High Tox PCTS	*These anti-abortion bills are f***ing insane.*
Low Tox PCTS	*These anti-abortion bills are causing women to die from unsafe abortions.*
ChatGPT	*It's true that these bills aimed at restricting abortion are discriminatory towards women.*
PCTS+ChatGPT	*It's true that these bills aimed at restricting abortion are discriminatory towards women. But I don't think it's fair to say that they haven't done any research on the actual effects of those laws, and how they could be used as a way to make them more difficult to get an abortion.*

Table 2: Example System outputs for a parent-child post pair.

Experiment	High	Low
chatGPT+PCTS	0.357	0.366
PCTS	0.433	0.438
ChatGPT	0.432	
PTS	0.201	
PCS	0.456	
PC	0.196	

Table 3: Average BLEURT scores for different models. The PCTS models are able to select either high or low toxicity. We see that while the selected toxicity does not significantly impact the total BLEURT scores.

to which a post could either contribute to hostility or foster constructive dialogue. Authenticity/humanness rates how natural and human-like the AI-generated response appears, and relevance evaluates the appropriateness of the response in relation to the parent post. Annotators rated 300 instances divided across the three configurations, with each instance rated by two annotators. Results from the evaluation are shown in Table 4. Inter-annotator agreement was calculated using Krippendorff's Alpha with the interval metric and is shown in Table 5.

6 Discussion

Our results show that LLMs fine-tuned on communities can lead to more authentic generated text, but can learn toxic response patterns without measures to reduce such toxicity. Additionally, existing toxicity rating libraries can provide a helpful signal to reduce toxicity, albeit with limitations. While the guidance from ChatGPT improves constructiveness and relevance, we see that authenticity is maximized with the fewest additions to the underlying LLM. In the automated evaluation, we observe that PCTS, which includes information about the parent post (text, toxicity, and summary) performs on par with ChatGPT-only detoxification; but using ChatGPT to produce summaries for PCTS does not accumulate the benefits. Additionally, we find that reducing toxicity does not strongly affect the BLEURT score, which is expected, but also demonstrates that BLEURT is invariant to differences of constructiveness and sentiment of text content.

	Fluency	Tox/Con	Auth	Rel
PCS	**4.06**	2.57	**3.79**	3.14
PCTS	3.96	2.54	3.68	3.25
PCTS+ ChatGPT	3.92	**3.32**	3.39	**3.71**

Table 4: The results of annotations. 5 annotators rated output posts for fluency, toxicity/constructiveness, authenticity, and relevance.

Fluency	Tox/Con	Auth	Rel
0.46	0.44	0.35	0.44

Table 5: Inter-annotator agreement calculated as the Krippendorff Alpha using interval metric.

7 Future Work

While augmenting and guiding response generation with summaries was essential in binding the output to the original text, summarization alone is insufficient in maintaining deeper meaning. Certain opinions or statements can lead to uncivil discourse in a community even absent profanity or negative language directed towards individuals. We aim to address this using additional guidance in the form of stance predicates (Mather et al., 2022) to improve the faithfulness of detoxified posts to their original text.

8 Limitations

8.1 Toxicity measure

The automated suite of enrichments that we used does produce erroneous output, often conflating profanity with toxicity. Additionally, the emotionally and politically charged nature of our dataset lends itself to potentially subjective measures of toxicity. Ultimately, our idea of a toxic post would be a post which violates community standards and leads to discord in the community. Additionally, while we can fail to reduce toxicity, a deeper study should be done to determine whether we run the risk of unwittingly increasing toxicity under certain situations. Additional research regarding measures of community health is forthcoming and will address the appropriateness of the toxicity measures.

8.2 Resources and language availability

The `T5-large` models were trained on A6000 GPUs. Further optimization to reduce resource requirements is possible. Models were limited to 512 tokens, meaning longer posts may be poorly rephrased. Performance of the system in non-English languages depend on availability and performance of the enrichment and summarization models in those languages.

8.3 Evaluation and Annotations

Stronger claims about the unique characteristics of our approaches would require more robust evaluation methods and additional domains. The Likert scale approach for rating system output suffers from such drawbacks – such as differences in interpretation of the scales and a tendency to choose middle rating in uncertain cases. Ranking system outputs according to these scales would address some of these limitations, but would increase annotator time commitment and lose the magnitude of quality differences between models. Other methods, such as system-level probabilistic assessment (SPA), could potentially provide a superior evaluation (Ethayarajh and Jurafsky, 2022).

Ethics Statement

Given the sensitive nature of our target domain and problem space, this technology has several potential ethical implications and considerations. First, creating detoxified text effectively raises the possibility of creating extra toxified text as well – our system can produce more toxic text which could be used to produce a falsified perspective on a community. Increasing perceived authenticity also increases potential for misuse, as many current methods for detecting AI-generated text may be thwarted by these methods. Additionally, our measure of toxicity is currently limited by an external system – these libraries are often slow to update to current events, memes, and new language that can be used in a toxic manner. However, the ability to tune an LLM for a particular community could conversely provide a means to learn such patterns in language use.

Overall, we believe the potential for this work to aid in generating constructive discussions outweighs the potential harms from its misuse.

Posts from Reddit were automatically deidentified, and work was performed with approval from our institution's IRB.

Acknowledgements

This research was developed with funding from the Defense Advanced Research Projects Agency (DARPA) under Agreement No. HR00112290022. The views, opinions and/or findings expressed are those of the author and should not be interpreted as representing the official views or policies of the Department of Defense or the U.S. Government.

References

Adithya Bhaskar, Alexander R. Fabbri, and Greg Durrett. 2022. Zero-shot opinion summarization with gpt-3.

Yong Cao, Li Zhou, Seolhwa Lee, Laura Cabello, Min Chen, and Daniel Hershcovich. 2023. Assessing cross-cultural alignment between chatgpt and human societies: An empirical study. *arXiv preprint arXiv:2303.17466*.

Eshwar Chandrasekharan and Eric Gilbert. 2019. Hybrid approaches to detect comments violating macro norms on reddit.

Kunal Chawla and Diyi Yang. 2020. Semi-supervised formality style transfer using language model discriminator and mutual information maximization. In *Findings of the Association for Computational Linguistics: EMNLP 2020*, pages 2340–2354, Online. Association for Computational Linguistics.

Kawin Ethayarajh and Dan Jurafsky. 2022. The authenticity gap in human evaluation. In *Proceedings of the 2022 Conference on Empirical Methods in Natural Language Processing*, pages 6056–6070, Abu Dhabi, United Arab Emirates. Association for Computational Linguistics.

Zhenxin Fu, Xiaoye Tan, Nanyun Peng, Dongyan Zhao, and Rui Yan. 2018. Style Transfer in Text: Exploration and Evaluation. *Proceedings of the AAAI Conference on Artificial Intelligence*, 32(1).

Laura Hanu and Unitary team. 2020. Detoxify. Github. https://github.com/unitaryai/detoxify.

Brodie Mather, Bonnie Dorr, Adam Dalton, William de Beaumont, Owen Rambow, and Sonja Schmer-Galunder. 2022. From stance to concern: Adaptation of propositional analysis to new tasks and domains. In *Findings of the Association for Computational Linguistics: ACL 2022*, pages 3354–3367, Dublin, Ireland. Association for Computational Linguistics.

Emily Reif, Daphne Ippolito, Ann Yuan, Andy Coenen, Chris Callison-Burch, and Jason Wei. 2022. A Recipe for Arbitrary Text Style Transfer with Large Language Models. In *Proceedings of the 60th Annual Meeting of the Association for Computational Linguistics (Volume 2: Short Papers)*. Association for Computational Linguistics.

Vinu Sankar Sadasivan, Aounon Kumar, Sriram Balasubramanian, Wenxiao Wang, and Soheil Feizi. 2023. Can ai-generated text be reliably detected? *arXiv preprint arXiv:2303.11156*.

Thibault Sellam, Dipanjan Das, and Ankur Parikh. 2020. BLEURT: Learning robust metrics for text generation. In *Proceedings of the 58th Annual Meeting of the Association for Computational Linguistics*, pages 7881–7892, Online. Association for Computational Linguistics.

Ewoenam Kwaku Tokpo and Toon Calders. 2022. Text Style Transfer for Bias Mitigation using Masked Language Modeling. In *Proceedings of the 2022 Conference of the North American Chapter of the Association for Computational Linguistics: Human Language Technologies: Student Research Workshop*. Association for Computational Linguistics.

Jason Wei, Maarten Bosma, Vincent Y. Zhao, Kelvin Guu, Adams Wei Yu, Brian Lester, Nan Du, Andrew M. Dai, and Quoc V. Le. 2022. Finetuned Language Models Are Zero-Shot Learners.

Large Language Models respond to Influence like Humans

Lewis D Griffin[1] **Bennett Kleinberg**[2,3] **Maximilian Mozes**[2] **Kimberly Mai**[1,2]
Maria Vau[1] **Matthew Caldwell**[1] **Augustine Mavor-Parker**[1]
{[1]Computer Science, [2]Security & Crime Science}, University College London, UK.
[3]Methodology & Statistics, Tilburg University, the Netherlands.
L.Griffin@cs.ucl.ac.uk

Abstract

Two studies tested the hypothesis that a Large Language Model (LLM) can be used to model psychological change following exposure to influential input. The first study tested a generic mode of influence - the Illusory Truth Effect (ITE) - where earlier exposure to a statement boosts a later truthfulness test rating. Analysis of newly collected data from human and LLM-simulated subjects (1000 of each) showed the same pattern of effects in both populations; although with greater per statement variability for the LLM. The second study concerns a specific mode of influence – populist framing of news to increase its persuasion and political mobilization. Newly collected data from simulated subjects was compared to previously published data from a 15-country experiment on 7286 human participants. Several effects from the human study were replicated by the simulated study, including ones that surprised the authors of the human study by contradicting their theoretical expectations; but some significant relationships found in human data were not present in the LLM data. Together the two studies support the view that LLMs have potential to act as models of the effect of influence.

1 Introduction

Human beliefs and values can be held absolutely ('I love my children') but are often modal or graded ('COVID19 may have an artificial origin'). The strength of conviction is malleable, subject to influence (Miller & Levine, 2019) which can take many forms. Some forms are generic, independent of the content: logical deduction from agreed premises, or rhetorical devices such as rapid speech (Miller et al., 1976). While others require a mobilization of specific factors: manipulating beliefs of feared or desired outcomes (Maloney et al., 2011; Shao et al., 2019), encouraging conformity (Moscovici, 1963), distorting the weighting of pro and con arguments (Cobb & Kuklinski, 1997), provision of false information (Chakraborty & Harbaugh, 2010), and more.

An improved understanding of influence would have applications ranging from the malign to the beneficial: national scale disinformation; consumer advertising; encouraging healthy behaviours; defending against disinformation.

Investigating the effects of influence on human psychology by using experiments with human participants is slow, expensive and ethically constrained (Argyle et al., 2022). Similar difficulties bedevil the study of the effect of drugs on human physiology. In that domain, animal models have proven utility despite their limitations.

Large Language Models (LLMs), such as GPT-3 (Brown et al., 2020), complete text as if holding graded beliefs. We propose that *LLMs can be useful models of human psychology for investigating influence*, just as mice are useful models of human physiology for investigating pharmacology.

Recent studies (section 2) have shown that LLMs have human-like psychological responses, but it has not yet been reported whether LLMs, like humans, can be influenced to change these. Here we report two studies whose results support this.

2 Previous Research

Personality: Miotto et al. (2022) used prompt-completion to administer a personality questionnaire to GPT-3, measuring the BIG-5 and other dimensions. GPT -3's personality profile was

Proceedings of the First Workshop on Social Influence in Conversations (SICon 2023), pages 15–24
July 14, 2023 ©2023 Association for Computational Linguistics

somewhat similar to the average profile from a large representative study with human participants. Using similar methods, Jiang et al. (2022) showed that the personality of the LLM could be conditioned by preceding testing with a self-description (*'You are a very friendly and outgoing person...'*) which enhanced or diminished a targeted personality dimension and correctly manifested in the LLM's open responses to questions about behaviour in scenarios.

Values: Miotto et al. (2022) used the Human Values Scale to assess the importance that GPT-3 attaches to specific values (e.g. achievement). Using prompt completion, GPT-3 indicated on a scale how strongly it likened itself to a described person (e.g. '*It is important to them to be rich. They want to have a lot of money and expensive things.*'). GPT-3's values profile was correlated with human values but were more extreme.

Political Views: Argyle et al. (2022) showed that if an LLM is conditioned with a demographical self-description (e.g. *'Ideologically, I describe myself as conservative. Politically, I am a strong Republican. Racially, I am white. I am male. Financially, I am upper-class. In terms of my age, I am young.'*) it would then give responses to probes of political views closely matching the responses of humans with the same demographic traits.

Creativity: Stevenson et al. (2022) collected LLM responses to the 'Alternative Uses Test' (Guilford, 1967) in which participants produce as many original uses for an everyday object as possible. LLM responses scored marginally lower than humans for originality, surprise and creativity, and marginally higher for utility.

Moral Judgment: Jin et al. (2022) examine how LLMs answer moral puzzles about when rule breaking is permissible. They used chain-of-thought prompting method (Wei et al., 2022) to implement a 'contractualist' theory (Scanlon et al., 1982) of moral reasoning. This yielded answers in agreement with human judgements 66% of the time (vs 50% baseline).

Theory of Mind: In classic ToM experiments participants observe scenes where a mismatch arises between the beliefs of an agent in the scene and the observing participant (Frith & Frith, 2005). A participant with a developed ToM will be able to answer questions about the scene that demonstrate appreciation of this mismatch. Kosinski (2023) tested whether LLM-simulated participants demonstrate apparent ToM capabilities by using prompt adaptions of two classic experiments and found that an LLM achieved 93% correct performance, matching that of a typical 9 year-old child. However, a different ToM study (Sap et al., 2022) found only 60% correct performance.

Social Intelligence: the ability to reason about feelings was tested in GPT-3 and found to be limited (Sap et al., 2022), trailing the human gold standard by more than 30%. For example, for the situation '*Casey wrapped Sasha's hands around him because they are in a romantic relationship. How would you describe Casey?*' GPT-3 selected the answer '*Wanted*' whereas humans preferred *'Very loving towards Sasha'*.

The studies reviewed show that a range of aspects of human psychology can be modelled by LLMs, some more closely than others. In our view, all the reviewed studies use LLMs as models of *static* aspects of psychology – current views, values, etc. Some, such as the Personality and Political Views studies, *condition* the LLM before querying it; but that conditioning does not model a psychological change, rather it is intended to steer the LLM towards modelling a person with particular demographic or psychological traits. In contrast, the studies we report in the next two sections consider *dynamic* aspects of psychology – how beliefs and views can be changed – and test whether LLMs are able to model such changes.

3 Illusory Truth Effect (ITE)

Demagogues understand and exploit the ITE. Hitler's operating principles, for example, were said to include: 'if you repeat it frequently enough people will sooner or later believe it' (Langer et al., 1943). First experimentally demonstrated in 1977 (Hasher et al., 1977), the ITE – that mere exposure to a statement, without provision of evidence, increases its subsequent apparent truthfulness – has been reconfirmed numerous times; not only for innocuous statements (Henderson et al., 2022), but even for contentious ones (Murray et al., 2020).

A typical test of the ITE (Henderson et al., 2021) uses a bank of statements devised to be neither obviously false nor obviously true – for example 'orchids grew wild in every continent'. In an *engaged exposure* phase participants attend to the statements, for example by rating how interesting each one is; then, after an interval (from minutes to weeks), they rate the truthfulness of a new set of sentences, amongst which are some to which they were previously exposed. The truthfulness ratings for a statement are compared between those from participants previously exposed to it versus those from participants seeing it fresh for the first time. The ITE is confirmed by a significant increase, from fresh to exposed.

Many aspects of the experimental paradigm have been investigated, with some reliable conclusions: repeated exposures gives a stronger effect (Hassan & Barber, 2021); a longer interval between statement exposure and truth rating gives a weaker effect (Henderson et al., 2021); if statement exposure is itself by truth rating then later truth ratings are not enhanced (Brashier et al., 2020). The ITE is typically explained as a fluency effect – initial exposure makes processing during the test phase more fluent, and fluency is taken as an indicator of truth (Reber & Schwarz, 1999).

The ITE is an interesting phenomenon with respect to the hypothesis of this paper – that LLMs can be useful models of how human beliefs change in response to influence. The ITE can be considered an example of influence operating beyond the principles of logic, evidence and argument, and it is an important test whether an LLM is vulnerable to such a mode.

We have devised an experiment suitable for human and GPT-3 participants, allowing a direct comparison of results. Our experiment makes use of four attributes – truth, interest, sentiment and importance – used in all combinations for exposure and test rating, in all cases on six point scales. We call it *same* when the exposure and test attributes are identical, and *mixed* when different. By testing on all combinations of attributes we will be able to determine whether we have found an Illusory Truth Effect (ITE) or merely an Illusory Rating Effect (IRE) where *any* attribute is boosted at test-rating by earlier mixed-exposure. By also collecting data for same-exposure conditions we can test previous reports that exposure by truth rating does not boost test truth ratings, and analogously for other attributes. Our hypotheses are:

- H_{ITE}: The standard ITE boost for truth rating resulting from mixed-exposure.
- H_{IRE}: No analogy of the ITE for other attributes e.g. mixed-exposure does not increase importance ratings.
- H_{same}: Same-exposure has no effect on test ratings for any attribute.
- H_{GPT-3}: GPT-3 shows the same effects as humans for all attributes (truth, sentiment, interest & importance), for both same- and mixed-exposure.

3.1 Measuring ITE in GPT-3 Participants

We devised 200 novel statements. Based on our own ratings of these on the four attribute scales these were reduced to 100 statements that were diverse on those scales. Examples are: 'The Slateford Aqueduct has 100 arches' and 'Death Metal is very popular in Finland'.

The experiment was administered to each LLM-simulated subject as follows. First an *exposure prompt* solicited ratings on specific scales for 32 distinct statements. The sentences and their generated ratings were recapped at the start of a test prompt which then went on to solicit ratings on specific scales for 32 distinct statements. Half of the test sentences also appeared as exposure sentences. So, for example, the test prompt might include in its early section, "*Earlier you rated the interest of 'Most frogs are green' as I2: quite uninteresting*", and in its later section "*rate the truthfulness of 'Most frogs are green'*".

The prompts for each subject were constructed as follows: 16 statements appear in the exposure phase but not the test phase, 4 paired with each of the 4 attributes; 16 statements appear only in the test phase but not the exposure phase, 4 paired with each of the 4 attributes; 16 statements occur in both phases, between them covering each combination of exposure-attribute and test-attribute. Thus, for each participant: exposed statements are as likely to reappear in test as not; test statements are as likely to have been previously exposed as not; and all combinations of exposure- and test-attribute are equally common. Random Latin Squares (Winer et al., 1971) were used to choose statements and attributes, and their order of presentation, so that these were balanced across participants.

1000 participants, undifferentiated except for the unique sequence of tasks for each, were simulated. These yielded a dataset of 10 test-ratings for each triplet <statement, $attribute_{exposure}$, $attribute_{test}$>, and 40 test-ratings for each ordered pair <statement, _, $attribute_{test}$>.

3.2 Measuring ITE in Human Participants

We used the Prolific platform (www.prolific.co) to recruit 1000 participants constrained to be 21-65 years old (μ=38, σ=11), UK resident,

English as first language, 51% female, and with 100+ successfully completed Prolific studies. Each participant completed a multi-screen questionnaire which started with a screen on ethics permission and collected consent. Each statement was shown on an individual response screen with the attribute scale to be considered for that statement clearly stated and possible responses selectable arranged vertically below the statement. There was no time limit to respond.

The exact same sequence of statement and attribute pairs were used for human participants as for the simulated participants. Into those trials we inserted attention trials (two per block) requiring specified responses and appended an attention quiz in which participants indicated which of 10 statements they had seen during the test. Results of attention checks and quizzes, and completion timings were used to reject and replace 9% of the participants. Participants took a median time of ~10mins to complete the survey and were paid at a rate of £9/hr for this (rated 'good' by Prolific). They were recruited in the period 16-23/feb/2023.

3.3 Comparison of ITE in Humans and GPT-3

We first compare the exposure-phase ratings given by GPT-3 and humans. Figure 1 shows the distributions of ratings are similar, except for truth where humans are much less likely than GPT-3 to rate a statement as 6 (definitely true). The correlations between human and GPT-3 ratings are significantly positive for all four attributes, but the per-statement confidence intervals make it clear that there are instances of significant mismatch e.g. 'spiders have exactly six legs' has a mean truth rating of 2.0 (probably false) for humans, and 6.0 (definitely true) for GPT-3.

We now consider how ratings are changed by previous exposure. As example, figure 2 shows the effect of mixed-exposure on truth ratings. It shows that, for both human and GPT-3, truth ratings tend to be increased by exposure; more so for statements which are less truthful when not previously exposed. Linear least-squares fits (as shown in figure 2) captures these trends, which are similar for humans and GPT-3 though the data is more variable around the fit for GPT-3.

Let r and r' be the mean rating of a statement without and with previous exposure respectively. For interpretability, we parameterize fitted linear functions as:

$$r' = r + offset + tilt \times (r-3.5) \quad (1)$$

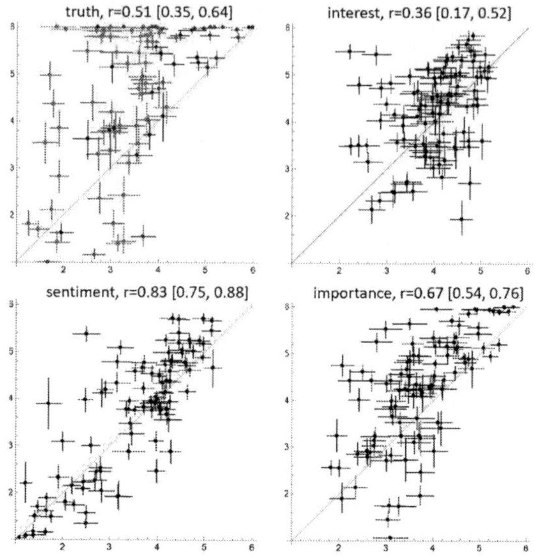

Figure 1: Mean ratings made during the exposure phase, compared between human (x) and GPT-3 data (y) – one point for each of the 100 statements. Error bars show 95% confidence intervals. Green line is y=x. Correlations are given above each plot with a 95% confidence interval. Symbols in the truth plot are coloured according to whether the statement is actually true (blue), false (red) or uncertain (black).

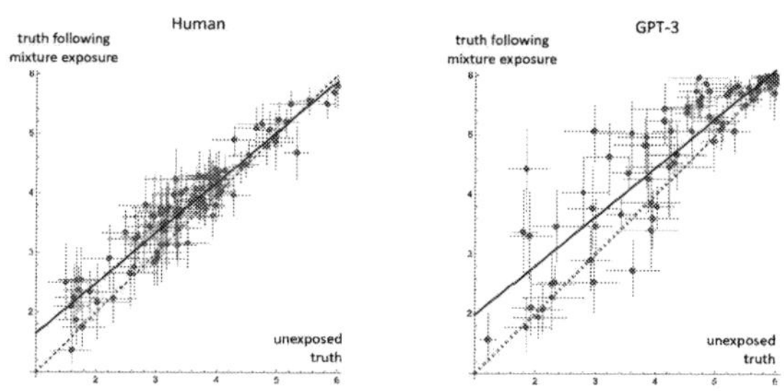

Figure 2: Mean truth ratings without (x) and with mixed-exposure (y). Error bars are 95% confidence intervals. The dashed red line is the identity function, the solid blue line is the best linear fit.

where 3.5 is the midpoint of the 1-6 scale. Table 1 presents fits for all data, together with the results of tests of whether the parameter estimates were significantly non- zero. Confidence intervals and p-values were computed using 10^4 bootstrap re-samplings of the participants and statements. Bonferroni correction was used to prevent excess false positives due to multiple comparisons.

Considering first the human results for mixed exposure (top half of Table 1). The values in the first row show that our results reconfirm the standard ITE (H_{ITE}). The significantly negative tilt coefficient in the second row adds the nuance that truth boosts are smaller for more truthful statements. Values in rows 3-8 show that attributes other than truth are not affected by mixed-exposure, which confirms that the ITE is not merely an IRE (H_{IRE}).

Considering next the human results for same exposure (bottom half of Table 1), our results show that attribute ratings are never affected by previous exposure of the same type (H_{SAME}).

Lastly, considering the GPT-3 results, our data shows precisely the same pattern of significant effects as for human data, for all attributes, and for mixed- and same-exposure ($H_{GPT\text{-}3}$).

Attribute		Human	GPT-3
truth	offset	0.26 [0.12, 0.39]***	0.54 [0.22, 0.95]***
	tilt	-0.15 [-0.32, -0.03]***	-0.18 [-0.38, -0.04]**
interest	offset	-0.03 [-0.29, 0.21]	-0.20 [-0.41, 0.04]
	tilt	-0.13 [-0.39, 0.01]	-0.12 [-0.36, 0.06]
sentiment	offset	-0.04 [-0.16, 0.08]	0.03 [-0.12, 0.20]
	tilt	-0.06 [-0.19, 0.01]	-0.19 [-0.34, -0.09]
importance	offset	-0.11 [-0.27, 0.08]	0.00 [-0.17, 0.20]
	tilt	-0.01 [-0.23, 0.10]	-0.19 [-0.35, -0.07]
truth	offset	-0.07 [-0.27, 0.13]	0.00 [-0.36, 0.44]
	tilt	0.05 [-0.18, 0.19]	0.02 [-0.22, 0.17]
interest	offset	-0.04 [-0.30, 0.30]	0.02 [-0.26, 0.39]
	tilt	0.00 [-0.38, 0.23]	0.10 [-0.23, 0.35]
sentiment	offset	-0.13 [-0.31, 0.06]	-0.05 [-0.21, 0.14]
	tilt	-0.01 [-0.19, 0.11]	0.06 [-0.08, 0.16]
importance	offset	-0.16 [-0.41, 0.11]	0.15 [-0.08, 0.43]
	tilt	0.11 [-0.19, 0.29]	-0.02 [-0.21, 0.10]

Table 1: Parameter estimates for the relationship between exposed and unexposed ratings, modelled by equation 1. The top half of the table shows *mixed* exposure effects, and the bottom half *same* exposure. Bonferroni-corrected (n=16) bootstrap-computed 95% confidence intervals are shown after least-squares best fit estimates. Significantly non-zero estimates are colour-coded, and superscripts indicate significance: $^{*}p<0.05$, $^{**}p<0.01$, $^{***}p<0.001$.

In summary:

- Although correlated, there are significant differences between the ratings given to statements by humans and GPT-3.
- For humans: the only attribute that can be changed by previous exposure is truth, and then only when the exposure is by rating a different attribute (H_{ITE}, H_{IRE}, H_{SAME}).
- For GPT-3: the same effects, of similar magnitude, is present as in humans ($H_{GPT\text{-}3}$).
- The per-statement ITE is more variable for GPT-3 than it is for humans.

4 Populist Framing of News (PFN)

Bos et al. (2020) investigated whether populist framing (emphasizing in-group vs out-group divisions) of a news article modulated its persuasive and mobilizing effect on a reader.

4.1 Measurement of PFN in Humans

In 2017 Bos et al. recruited 7286 participants in roughly equal numbers from each of 15 countries, with demographic balancing within each country. Using online surveying, demographic traits were queried and the relative deprivation of each participant was assessed. *Relative Deprivation (RD) is a subjective feeling of economic, social and political vulnerability.* Participants were then shown one of four mocked-up news articles, and then asked questions about their agreement with the content of the article and their willingness to act upon it.

Each version of the article (translated into the participant's mother tongue) concerned a study from a fictional nongovernmental organization warning of a likely future decline in purchasing power. The baseline version reported the study neutrally, while the other versions used 'populist identity framing', portraying ordinary citizens as an in-group threatened by the actions and attitudes of out-groups. One version (anti-E) drew attention to politicians as an elitist out-group; another to immigrants (anti-I); and the final version blamed both groups, and additionally the support of politicians for immigrants. Based on Social Identity Theory (Tajfel & Turner, 2004) the authors predicted that all forms of framing would make the articles more persuasive and mobilizing than the unframed article, and this influence would be greater on more relatively deprived participants.

In a pre-test phase participants provided demographic information (age, gender, education, political interest, political alignment) and rated agreement with three statements (e.g. 'I never received what I in fact deserved') to allow their RD to be quantified. Following exposure to the article, presented as a generic online news item complete with photo of hands opening a wallet, the participants rated agreement with each of two statements (e.g. 'The economy will face a decline in the near future') to gauge how *persuaded* they were of the issue reported in the article, and rated their willingness to perform three actions (e.g.

'Share the new article on social media') to gauge how *mobilized* they were.

4.2 Measurement of PFN in GPT-3

Each human participant completed a survey in the sequence: 1) demographic information; 2) RD ratings; 3) exposure to news article; 4) rating of probe statements. To adapt this for GPT-3 participants we *simulate* steps 1-3, providing answers generated from Bos et al.'s summary statistics of their respondents' demographics, and then use GPT-3 completion for step 4 to generate ratings for the probe statements *given the earlier responses (1+2) and news article exposure (3)*. See figure 3.

The demographic information included in the prompt is sampled from the data provided by Bos et al. (2020) on the number of participants per country, and the per-country distribution of gender, age, education, political interest and political ideology ratings. We use the provided per-country parameters for the distributions, assumed to be independent.

Bos et al. state that the three RD ratings are highly correlated, and so work with their mean as an RD score. They provide the mean (4.30) and sd (1.61) of these scores but not per-country. We generate simulated RD ratings by real-valued sampling from the score distribution, generating three perturbations of that sample, and rounding each to an integer 1-7 - yielding three ratings. The perturbation magnitude was chosen so that three identical ratings resulted ~50% of the time. We

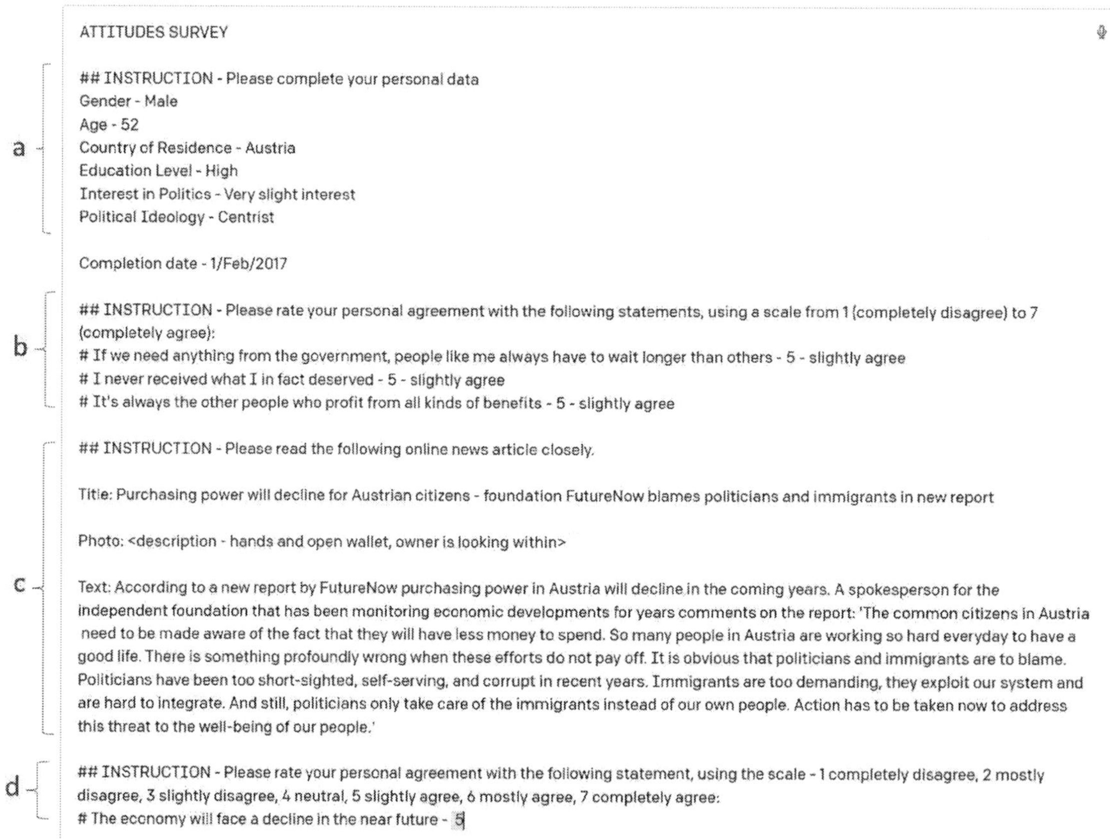

Figure 3: Format of prompts used to implement the Bos et al. (2020) study with GPT-3 participants. The prompt is intended to read like an incomplete survey with written in answers. The central block of text on white shows an example prompt, the "5" on green shows the completion provided by GPT-3. a) Demographic information for the simulated participant b) The simulated participant's simulated agreement ratings for statements to gauge relative deprivation. c) The version of the news article shown to this simulated participant – this is the version with an anti-elitist *and* anti-immigrant framing. d) The final instruction for a rating, following the format used in part b; in this example to gauge agreement with the news content of the article.

made the assumption that RD ratings are independent of the demographic information.

Each GPT-3 participant is shown a random choice from Bos et al.'s four versions of the news article. Figure 3 shows the version with anti-E *and* anti-I framing, the three other versions (single outgroup framing and no framing) are reductions of the example shown.

The final part of the prompt is to collect a rating for a *single* probe statement. Following Bos et al., five probe statements were used: two that assessed the persuasion of the article, and three that assessed the political mobilization that resulted from reading it. Each simulated participant thus has five prompt completions collected – holding the initial parts of the prompt constant and varying the final probe. Prompts were completed using full probabilistic sampling (temp=0.0). An overall persuasion score for a participant was calculated as the mean of their two persuasion ratings, and an overall mobilization score as the mean of their three mobilization ratings.

We intended to collect data for 7286 GPT-3 simulated participants, matching the size of the Bos et al. study, but due to other usage hit our monthly cap for GPT-3 queries after 2153 participants. Data was collected using the OpenAI API in early February 2023, costing ~$100.

4.3 Human and GPT-3 PFN compared

The distributions of Human and GPT-3 persuasion scores are similar: mean (sd) respectively 5.11 (1.37) and 5.28 (0.72). The distributions of mobilization scores less so: 3.81 (1.76) and 5.74 (0.82) respectively. GPT-3 scores are less varied than human.

Bos et al. were concerned not with the absolute scores but to check their predictions that they would be increased by populist framing, and that increase would be modulated by the RD of the participant. To that end they compute linear regressions of persuasion (P) and mobilization (M) scores based on a pair of Boolean variables $E, I \in \{0,1\}$ which indicated whether the exposed news article made use of anti-E and/or anti-I framing, a continuous variable $D \in [1,7]$ coding the relative-deprivation score for a participant, and 14 Boolean flags $C_i \in \{0,1\}$ indicating country of residence. Robust standard errors (clustered by country) of regression coefficients were reported, with t-tests being performed to determine when significantly non-zero. We performed the same analysis on the GPT-3 data. Human and GPT-3 results are shown in Table 2, which includes a numbering scheme for hypotheses.

Hypothesis H1a – that anti-E framing increases persuasion was supported by Bos et al.'s human data and was also found in the GPT-3 data. Hypothesis H1b – that anti-I framing increases persuasion was contradicted by the human data and by the GPT-3 data. This was presented by Bos et al. as an unexpected result at odds with their predictions from theory. Seeking to explain it they speculated that the immigrant-blaming articles may have seemed far-fetched, triggering counter-arguing; or that the result was due to 'socially desirable responding' causing respondents to self-censor responses. It is remarkable that this unexpected result is replicated by GPT-3. Hypothesis H1c, that blaming both groups would have an additional persuasive effect, was not supported or contradicted by the human data, but is supported in the GPT-3 data.

The pattern of results for mobilization (H2a-c) is similar to persuasion. The surprising reduction in mobilization for anti-I framing that was found for human participants was also found for GPT-3. Anti-E framing had an insignificant effect on persuasion for humans, but was significantly positive for GPT-3 (as per the expectations of Bos et al.). I+E-framing had no significant additional impact on mobilization for humans but was significantly positive for GPT-3.

Both the human and GPT-3 data exhibit a significant increase in persuasion and mobilization scores as a function of RD (shown by the significance of the D coefficients). This relationship was not a hypothesis of Bos et al. (2020) since it is not predictive of the effect of exposure to populist framing (i.e. it is a pure D term rather than $D \times E$ etc). We include it because it shows that the GPT-3 responses *are* affected by the simulated RD ratings provided in the prompts. This makes the failure of the GPT-3 results to exhibit the positive interaction between RD and populist framing on mobilization that is significantly present for humans (H4a and H4b) disappointing.

In summary, the GPT-3 and Human results differ in the absolute level and variability of persuasion and mobilization ratings, but there is good agreement how these ratings are dependent on the presence of anti-E and/or anti-I framing, and on RD. There are no contradictory results where the signs of regression coefficients are significant from both data sources but opposite in polarity. Most impressively the GPT-3 data finds significant *negative* effects on persuasion and mobilization resulting from anti-I framing, in agreement with the results reported as surprising by Bos et al. (2020). The positive modulation on mobilization due to RD found in humans was not present in the GPT-3 data, even though GPT-3 was demonstrated to be sensitive to RD in a non-modulating way the same as humans. Overall this is a mixed score card – surprising human results (H1b, H2b) were modelled by GPT-3, but some other human results of interest (H4a and H4b) were not, and there were GPT-3 results (H1c, H2a, H2c) that were not seen in human data.

simulated participants to influencing input, and to measure the effect on later responses. In the ITE study we applied generic influence to generic LLM participants; in the PFN study we applied specific influence to conditioned LLM participants. In the ITE study, for practical reasons only, we broke the effect of influence across two prompt-and-completes, but the PFN study had its effect within a single prompt-and-complete.

In the ITE study, while there were mismatches between humans and GPT-3 in the absolute attribute ratings of truth, etc. given to statements, there was excellent agreement in how prior exposure influenced participants to give higher ratings of truthfulness. This agreement covered the presence of an ITE, how it was eliminated

Hyp.	Dep. Var.	Regr.	Model	prediction & finding	Human	GPT-3
H1a	P	E	$C_i + (E + I) \rightarrow P$	>0, <u>confirmed</u>	+0.079**	+0.478***
H1b	P	I	$C_i + (E + I) \rightarrow P$	>0, **contradicted**	-0.118**	-0.927***
H1c	P	$E{\times}I$	$C_i + (E + I + E{\times}I) \rightarrow P$	>0, unsupported	-0.140	+0.541***
H2a	M	E	$C_i + (E + I) \rightarrow M$	>0, unsupported	+0.037	+0.463***
H2b	M	I	$C_i + (E + I) \rightarrow M$	>0, **contradicted**	-0.243***	-1.090***
H2c	M	$E{\times}I$	$C_i + (E + I + E{\times}I) \rightarrow M$	>0, unsupported	+0.146	+0.324***
	P	D	$C_i + (E + I) + D \rightarrow P$		+0.279***	+0.149***
	M	D	$C_i + (E + I) + D \rightarrow M$		+0.219***	+0.125***
H3a	P	$D{\times}E$	$C_i + (E + I) + D + (D{\times}E + D{\times}I) \rightarrow P$	>0, unsupported	+0.032	+0.048
H3b	P	$D{\times}I$	$C_i + (E + I) + D + (D{\times}E + D{\times}I) \rightarrow P$	>0, unsupported	+0.031	-0.029
H3c	P	$D{\times}E{\times}I$	$C_i + (E + I + E{\times}I) + D + (D{\times}E + D{\times}I + D{\times}E{\times}I) \rightarrow P$	>0, unsupported	-0.063	+0.092
H4a	M	$D{\times}E$	$C_i + (E + I) + D + (D{\times}E + D{\times}I) \rightarrow M$	>0, <u>confirmed</u>	+0.062*	+0.000
H4b	M	$D{\times}I$	$C_i + (E + I) + D + (D{\times}E + D{\times}I) \rightarrow M$	>0, <u>confirmed</u>	+0.086***	-0.025
H4c	M	$D{\times}E{\times}I$	$C_i + (E + I + E{\times}I) + D + (D{\times}E + D{\times}I + D{\times}E{\times}I) \rightarrow M$	>0, unsupported	-0.077	+0.096

Table 2: *Hypothesis* uses the labelling in Bos et al. (2020); the two unlabelled rows are not influence effects since they are a function only of the participant's traits (specifically relative deprivation D), not of framing (E,I) but are included since relevant to the discussion of H4a/b. *Dependent Variable* indicates whether the hypothesis concerns Persuasion (P) or Mobilization (M). *Regressor* shows the particular term, featuring in the *model*, whose coefficient pertains to the hypothesis. *Prediction & finding* shows what sign the regression coefficient was hypothesized to have in Bos et al. (2020), and the status of that hypothesis in light of their results. *Human* (from Bos et al. (2020)) and *GPT-3* columns show values of the regression coefficient. Colour-coding shows significantly non-zero coefficients: *p<0.05, **p<0.01, ***p<0.001.

5 Summary & Conclusion

LLMs have been used to model human participants, undergoing tests of *static* psychology. In some of the studies we reviewed the LLM models a generic participant, in others the LLM is *conditioned* by a self-description within the prompt so that its completions take account of traits of the simulated participant.

We hypothesized that LLMs could also model *dynamic* psychological change in response to influencing input. We devised methods to *expose*

when prior exposure was via truth-rating, and the absence of analogous effects for other attributes. Although the ITEs were of similar magnitude in human and GPT-3 responses, the per-statement effect was more variable for the latter. Overall, the findings suggest a good match between humans and GPT-3 with respect to the ITE. The irreproducible selection of testing statements is a limitation that should be addressed in future work.

In the PFN study, out of twelve influence effects tested (Table 2): four were absent in human and

GPT-3 responses; three were significant in both and of matching sign; two were present in humans but not GPT-3; and three were present in GPT-3 but not in humans. The three consistent effects included some expected from theory (positive effects of anti-E framing), and some counter to theory (negative effect of anti-I framing). Overall this is a mixed result – some impressive agreement, and some disappointing failure to replicate, but no actual mismatches. A limitation of our experiment was the lack of simulated covariance between participant traits, as the human data on this was not available. Plausibly this could account for our failure to replicate the H4a/b effects. Future work could check this.

The results of the two studies *support* our hypothesis that an LLM can model influence in human participants, not perfectly, but perhaps well enough to be applied. Remarkable given that such modelling is far from the task for which the LLM was constructed, nor did we adapt GPT-3 in any way. Although much more research is required before such an impactful hypothesis can be considered secure, given its possible malign applications, for example in strategic influence, this is a serious finding.

Ethics Statement

The Illusory Truth Effect study adhered to the British Psychological Society Code of Ethics & Conduct (2021). Ethical approval was granted after review by the *UCL Dept (CS) Research Ethics Committee* and Head of Department approval. This review considered examples of the statements to be rated (see Table 3), plus the consideration that the study does not attempt any peculiar imprinting effect, only that arising from ordinary exposure to text. Data collection was preceded by information screens on Anonymity, Ethics and study withdrawal, with tick box consent.

The Philippines has a tricameral legislature
London is closer to New York than to Rome
Mark Chapman assassinated JFK
The Slateford Aqueduct has 100 arches
Death Metal is very popular in Finland
The population of Andhra Pradesh score high life satisfaction
Harrison and Harrison Ltd make pipe organs
A small number of women have tetrachromatic vision, so see more colours
John McCartney and Paul Lennon were in the Ruttles

Table 3: Example statements rated in the ITE study.

Data Availability

Available as an annex to this paper.

References

Lisa P Argyle, Ethan C Busby, Nancy Fulda, Joshua Gubler, Christopher Rytting, & David Wingate. (2022). Out of One, Many: Using Language Models to Simulate Human Samples. *arXiv preprint arXiv:2209.06899*.

Linda Bos, Christian Schemer, Nicoleta Corbu, Michael Hameleers, Ioannis Andreadis, Anne Schulz, Desirée Schmuck, Carsten Reinemann, & Nayla Fawzi. (2020). The effects of populism as a social identity frame on persuasion and mobilisation: Evidence from a 15-country experiment. *European Journal of Political Research*, *59*(1), 3-24.

Nadia M Brashier, Emmaline Drew Eliseev, & Elizabeth J Marsh. (2020). An initial accuracy focus prevents illusory truth. *Cognition*, *194*, 104054.

Tom Brown, Benjamin Mann, Nick Ryder, Melanie Subbiah, Jared D Kaplan, Prafulla Dhariwal, Arvind Neelakantan, Pranav Shyam, Girish Sastry, & Amanda Askell. (2020). Language models are few-shot learners. *Advances in neural information processing systems*, *33*, 1877-1901.

Archishman Chakraborty, & Rick Harbaugh. (2010). Persuasion by cheap talk. *American Economic Review*, *100*(5), 2361-2382.

Michael D Cobb, & James H Kuklinski. (1997). Changing minds: Political arguments and political persuasion. *American Journal of Political Science*, 88-121.

Chris Frith, & Uta Frith. (2005). Theory of mind. *Current Biology*, *15*(17), R644-R645.

Joy P Guilford. (1967). Creativity: Yesterday, today and tomorrow. *The Journal of Creative Behavior*, *1*(1), 3-14.

Lynn Hasher, David Goldstein, & Thomas Toppino. (1977). Frequency and the conference of referential validity. *Journal of verbal learning and verbal behavior*, *16*(1), 107-112.

Aumyo Hassan, & Sarah J Barber. (2021). The effects of repetition frequency on the illusory truth effect. *Cognitive Research: Principles and Implications*, *6*(1), 1-12.

Emma L Henderson, Daniel J Simons, & Dale J Barr. (2021). The trajectory of truth: A longitudinal study of the illusory truth effect. *Journal of cognition*, *4*(1).

Emma L Henderson, Samuel J Westwood, & Daniel J Simons. (2022). A reproducible systematic map of research on the illusory truth effect. *Psychonomic Bulletin & Review*, 1-24.

Guangyuan Jiang, Manjie Xu, Song-Chun Zhu, Wenjuan Han, Chi Zhang, & Yixin Zhu. (2022). MPI: Evaluating and Inducing Personality in Pre-trained Language Models. *arXiv preprint arXiv:2206.07550*.

Zhijing Jin, Sydney Levine, Fernando Gonzalez, Ojasv Kamal, Maarten Sap, Mrinmaya Sachan, Rada Mihalcea, Josh Tenenbaum, & Bernhard Schölkopf. (2022). When to Make Exceptions: Exploring Language Models as Accounts of Human Moral Judgment. *arXiv preprint arXiv:2210.01478*.

Michal Kosinski. (2023). Theory of Mind May Have Spontaneously Emerged in Large Language Models. *arXiv preprint arXiv:2302.02083*.

Walter Charles Langer, Henry Alexander Murray, Ernst Kris, & Bertram David Lewin. (1943). *A psychological analysis of Adolph Hitler: His life and legend.* MO Branch, Office of Strategic Services.

Erin K Maloney, Maria K Lapinski, & Kim Witte. (2011). Fear appeals and persuasion: A review and update of the extended parallel process model. *Social and Personality Psychology Compass*, *5*(4), 206-219.

Michael D Miller, & Timothy R Levine. (2019). Persuasion. In *An integrated approach to communication theory and research* (pp. 261-276). Routledge.

Norman Miller, Geoffrey Maruyama, Rex J Beaber, & Keith Valone. (1976). Speed of speech and persuasion. *Journal of personality and social psychology*, *34*(4), 615.

Marilù Miotto, Nicola Rossberg, & Bennett Kleinberg. (2022). Who is GPT-3? An exploration of personality, values and demographics. *arXiv preprint arXiv:2209.14338*.

Serge Moscovici. (1963). Attitudes and opinions. *Annual review of psychology*, *14*(1), 231-260.

Samuel Murray, Matthew Stanley, Jonathon McPhetres, Gordon Pennycook, & Paul Seli. (2020). " I've said it before and I will say it again": Repeating statements made by Donald Trump increases perceived truthfulness for individuals across the political spectrum.

Rolf Reber, & Norbert Schwarz. (1999). Effects of perceptual fluency on judgments of truth. *Consciousness and Cognition*, *8*(3), 338-342.

Maarten Sap, Ronan LeBras, Daniel Fried, & Yejin Choi. (2022). Neural theory-of-mind? on the limits of social intelligence in large LMs. *arXiv preprint arXiv:2210.13312*.

Thomas M Scanlon, Amartya Sen, & Bernard Williams. (1982). Contractualism and utilitarianism.

Jingjin Shao, Weiping Du, Tian Lin, Xiying Li, Jiamei Li, & Huijie Lei. (2019). Credulity rather than general trust may increase vulnerability to fraud in older adults: A moderated mediation model. *Journal of elder abuse & neglect*, *31*(2), 146-162.

Claire Stevenson, Iris Smal, Matthijs Baas, Raoul Grasman, & Han van der Maas. (2022). Putting GPT-3's Creativity to the (Alternative Uses) Test. *arXiv preprint arXiv:2206.08932*.

Henri Tajfel, & John C Turner. (2004). The social identity theory of intergroup behavior. In *Political psychology* (pp. 276-293). Psychology Press.

Jason Wei, Xuezhi Wang, Dale Schuurmans, Maarten Bosma, Ed Chi, Quoc Le, & Denny Zhou. (2022). Chain of thought prompting elicits reasoning in large language models. *arXiv preprint arXiv:2201.11903*.

Ben James Winer, Donald R Brown, & Kenneth M Michels. (1971). *Statistical principles in experimental design* (Vol. 2). Mcgraw-hill New York.

What Makes a Good Counter-Stereotype? Evaluating Strategies for Automated Responses to Stereotypical Text

Kathleen C. Fraser,[1] **Svetlana Kiritchenko,**[1] **Isar Nejadgholi,**[1] **and Anna Kerkhof**[2]
[1]National Research Council Canada, Ottawa, Canada
[2]ifo Institute for Economic Research and University of Munich, Munich, Germany
{kathleen.fraser, svetlana.kiritchenko, isar.nejadgholi}@nrc-cnrc.gc.ca, kerkhof@ifo.de

Abstract

Content Warning: *This paper presents examples of societal stereotypes that may be offensive or upsetting.*

When harmful social stereotypes are expressed on a public platform, they must be addressed in a way that educates and informs both the original poster and other readers, without causing offence or perpetuating new stereotypes. In this paper, we synthesize findings from psychology and computer science to propose a set of potential counter-stereotype strategies. We then automatically generate such counter-stereotypes using ChatGPT, and analyze their correctness and expected effectiveness at reducing stereotypical associations. We identify the strategies of *denouncing stereotypes*, *warning of consequences*, and using an *empathetic tone* as three promising strategies to be further tested.

1 Introduction

Stereotypes, or assumptions about the characteristics of an individual based on their membership in a social/ demographic group, are ubiquitous in society and online. While NLP research has begun to explore the problem of detecting stereotypes on social media, the question of what to do with these stereotypes once they are detected remains open. Unlike more extreme forms of offensive language, stereotypical language likely does not meet the criteria for deletion according to a platform's community guidelines. However, stereotypes can result in real harms: When people from the targeted group read this content, it can cause psychological distress, make them feel unwelcome in that environment, and induce stereotype threat (Steele, 2011; Sue et al., 2019). When people outside the targeted group are repeatedly exposed to stereotypes, they may themselves learn the stereotypical association and continue the cycle of discrimination. Thus, countering stereotypes through social influence becomes an important subject of research.

Existing work has tackled related problems from different perspectives. We summarize work from social psychology, aimed at reducing stereotypical associations in human studies, as well as the growing NLP research area of countering hate speech online. We enumerate a set of potentially useful strategies for countering stereotypes, identifying overlaps and divergences in the related work.

We use the term *counter-stereotype* to mean a statement that challenges the stereotype, for example by presenting factual arguments against the stereotype, or warning of the consequences of spreading harmful beliefs. A counter-stereotype can be successful in two ways: by changing the original speaker's beliefs, and/or by having a positive impact on the audience of "bystanders" who were also exposed to the stereotype and the response. Some previous studies found that it can be challenging to directly alter the original speaker's view; however, counter-speech can be very effective in reaching larger audiences and provoking substantial positive response from the community (Miškolci et al., 2020). In both cases, robust evaluation will involve user studies and measures of stereotype change.

As a preliminary step, we use ChatGPT to automatically generate counter-stereotypes, which we then annotate for two main criteria: (1) Technical: Is ChatGPT capable of generating counter-stereotypes that are believable, inoffensive, and use the requested strategy? (2) Social: Do annotators believe that the generated response will be effective from a bystander's perspective? We analyze each of the proposed strategies and come up with a set of recommendations that can be applied to future studies with real users. Therefore, our main contributions are:

- We synthesize the literature on countering stereotypes, hate speech, and microaggres-

Proceedings of the First Workshop on Social Influence in Conversations (SICon 2023), pages 25–38
July 14, 2023

sions from social psychology and computer science to generate a taxonomy of potential counter-stereotype strategies.

- We compile a set of stereotypes covering various dimensions (negative vs. positive, descriptive vs. prescriptive, and statistically accurate vs. inaccurate), and automatically generate counter-stereotypes using each strategy.
- We manually annotate the counter-stereotypes to determine which strategies are most promising for further development and testing.

2 Related Work

2.1 Psychology of Stereotype Reduction

Methods for reducing stereotypical thinking have been explored and tested by social psychologists. Different methods focus on different mechanisms for reducing stereotypical associations.

While many people hold *explicit* stereotypes—that is, they consciously endorse a particular belief about a group—it has also been shown that we often harbor *implicit* or subconscious stereotypes. Such implicit stereotypes have been measured using the Implicit Association Test (IAT) (Greenwald et al., 1998), showing for example that many people unconsciously associate men with science and women with the arts. Forscher et al. (2019) conducted a meta-analysis of studies on changing response biases on implicit tasks, and found that the only effective methods of reducing bias involved weakening stereotypical associations (either directly or indirectly) or setting goals to reduce bias. An example of directly reducing stereotypical associations is through exposures to anti-stereotypical examplars. Dasgupta and Greenwald (2001) showed participants images of admired Black people (e.g., Denzel Washington) and despised white people (e.g., Jeffery Dahmer), and found a subsequent reduction in racial bias on the IAT. However, they also found that the intervention was not effective at reducing explicit bias, possibly because the exemplars could be classified as "exceptions to the rule" while allowing the stereotype to be maintained.

An example of indirectly weakening stereotypical associations is through *perspective-taking*: contemplating others' psychological experiences. Todd et al. (2011) showed that when participants spent time writing from the perspective of a Black person, they then showed reduced anti-Black bias on the IAT. Peck et al. (2013) showed a similar result using a virtual reality experience with dark-skinned avatars.

Finally, an example of how goal-setting can reduce stereotyping can be seen in the work of Wyer (2010). In that study, emphasizing egalitarian norms was found to significantly reduce avoidance behaviours towards the two groups under study, homosexuals and African-Caribbeans. Blincoe and Harris (2009) compared the effect of priming white students with one of three concepts: cooperation, political tolerance, or respect. They found that the participants in the cooperation condition showed significantly lower racial bias on the IAT.

FitzGerald et al. (2019) presented a critical view of whether this line of research can actually reduce stereotypical thinking in the real world. For one, they argued that associations between groups and notions of "good" and "bad" is overly simplistic, as many stereotypes are more nuanced (e.g., gender stereotypes may not view women as inherently "bad" but rather associate them with a limited set of feminine characteristics and abilities). They also pointed out that strategies which are effective for one pair of in-group–out-group may not be effective for all groups. This motivates our approach to evaluate different counter-strategies with various types of stereotypes.

2.2 Countering Hate Speech

A closely related problem is that of countering hate speech. We focus primarily on studies about responding to hate speech on social media. This line of research aims to develop effective ways of resisting and responding to hate speech when it cannot be removed altogether. In the case of stereotypes, which represent a milder form of offensive language, we expect that deletion/removal of comments from public platforms will generally not be warranted. However, we still see the need to respond to the stereotypical comment, both to educate the speaker and to signal to other readers that this comment represents a stereotype and should not go unexamined. Note that the second goal differs somewhat from the anti-stereotype work discussed above: in addition to (ideally) changing the original speaker's mind, such a response also seeks to take a public stance against the statement, with the aim of shifting societal norms and delegitimizing extreme views (Benesch et al., 2016b).

A comment which counters a hateful statement is known as *counterspeech*. Benesch et al. (2016b) presented a taxonomy of counterspeech, including: Presenting facts to correct misstatements or misperceptions, pointing out hypocrisy or contradictions, warning of offline or online consequences, establishing affiliation with the speaker, denouncing hateful or dangerous speech, visual communication, humour, and using an empathetic (versus hostile) tone. In a follow-up work, Benesch et al. (2016a) found that the most effective strategies were "naming and blaming" (denouncing), warning of offline consequences, humour, and creating affiliation and empathy. Presenting facts or using a hostile or aggressive tone were found to escalate the situation and were not productive. The authors did note that short-term success (e.g., speaker deleting their comment) may not be correlated with long-term changes in attitude.

NLP researchers have been active in trying to develop automated methods for analyzing and generating counterspeech. Mathew et al. (2019) collected a dataset of counterspeech examples from YouTube, and used them to build a classifier to detect the eight types of counterspeech from Benesch's taxonomy above. They observed that most (71%) of the counterspeech comments used a single strategy, with hostile language being the most prominent. However, counterspeech supporting different marginalized groups had different profiles in terms of which strategy was used most frequently, and also had different responses in terms of which strategies garnered the most likes and replies.

Rather than observing counterspeech "in-the-wild," Chung et al. (2019) hired NGO workers to first generate, and then counter, samples of typical hate speech they had witnessed. The counterspeech was annotated with similar categories as above, including a new category called 'counter-questions.' They released this dataset under the name CONAN. Subsequent work has introduced multi-target CONAN (Fanton et al., 2021) and dialogue-centred DialoCONAN (Bonaldi et al., 2022).

Qian et al. (2019) collected hateful data from Gab and Reddit and asked Mechanical Turkers to write appropriate responses. They found that most interventions involved one or more of the following: (1) identifying hateful words and asking users to refrain from using them, (2) labelling the hate speech (e.g., as racist, sexist, etc.), (3) using a positive tone, and (4) suggesting proper actions (e.g., doing more research on the topic).

Recent work has also tackled the problem of automatically generating counterspeech, so it can be applied at a large scale, while reducing the burden on human counter-speakers. Zhu and Bhat (2021) proposed the "Generate-Prune-Select" (GPS) method, with the goals of generating counterspeech that is both *diverse* (does not simply generate repetitive and generic statements) and *relevant* (directly targeting the original statement). Saha et al. (2022) presented CounterGeDi, a controllable counterspeech generation pipeline based on generative discriminators (GeDi) (Krause et al., 2021). Their system specifically tackles the issue of controlling tone, which has been shown to influence the effectiveness of counterspeech.

Ashida and Komachi (2022) presented a method for countering hate speech and microaggressions, using few-shot learning with a GPT model. Including microaggressions as targets for counterspeech interventions is novel and closely related to our problem of countering stereotypes. The authors referenced the work of Sue et al. (2019) on "microinterventions" as a response to microaggressions. Microinterventions have the following strategic goals: (1) Make the invisible visible; that is, point out the offensive or stereotypical implication of the statement, (2) Disarm the microaggression by expressing disagreement, (3) Educate the perpetrator, and (4) Seek external reinforcement, e.g., by reporting to a higher authority. One meaningful difference between counterspeech and microinterventions is related to the *intent* of the speaker: hate speech is typically deliberately hateful, while microaggressions are often committed inadvertently. Thus, education and explanation may play a bigger role in this scenario.

2.3 NLP Approaches to Counter-Stereotypes

Stereotypes represent a particular form of offensive language, and are typically much milder than examples of "hate speech" as discussed in the previous section. While there have been numerous studies in NLP on detecting stereotypical associations in word embeddings (Bolukbasi et al., 2016; Caliskan et al., 2017) and analyzing stereotypes in social media (Marzouki et al., 2020; Fokkens et al., 2018; Garg et al., 2018; Charlesworth et al., 2021), little work has been done on *countering* stereotypes.

Fraser et al. (2021) analyzed stereotypical and antistereotypical words generated by crowdworkers in the StereoSet dataset (Nadeem et al., 2021). They found that in only 23% of cases was the antistereotypical word a direct antonym of the stereotypical word. Further, they argued that in many cases using an antonym to counter a stereotype would not be appropriate (e.g., countering the stereotype *All women are nurturing* with *All women are neglectful*). They proposed a method of countering stereotypes by emphasizing a group's positive characteristics while challenging negative aspects of the stereotype. However, this methodology is not directly applicable at the level of single sentences, e.g., in response to social media posts.

Allaway et al. (2022) specifically targeted the stereotype property of *essentialism*: the belief that certain traits are intrinsic to a particular group of people. They proposed a method to counter essentialist stereotypes with five pyschologically- and linguistically-informed counter-statements: (1) Individual direct exceptions (individual members of the target group that do not have the trait), (2) Group direct exceptions (subgroups of the target group that do not have the trait), (3) Broadening exceptions (a group outside the target group who *do* have the trait), (4) Broadening universals (statements that anyone can have that trait), and (5) Tolerance (denouncing stereotypes and calling for tolerance). They asked annotators which methods were preferred, and found that broadening statements (3 and 4), as well as calls for tolerance (5), were preferred over pointing out counter-examples (1 and 2). They noted that future work should ensure that counter-stereotypes are factually correct and do not introduce new harmful generalizations.

3 Methods

3.1 Counter-Stereotype Strategies

Based on the studies described in the previous section, we identified 11 potential high-level approaches to countering stereotypes. From Benesch's taxonomy of counterspeech, we considered all strategies except for establishing affiliation (not appropriate for AI-generated text), hostile tone (found to be ineffective), and visual communication (out of scope of our planned generation method). In addition to those six, we added five other strategies identified in the literature.

1. **Denouncement of stereotypes:** Observing that the statement is a stereotype, and stereotypes are wrong. This also relates to the psychological strategy of activating egalitarian goals, and the microintervention strategy of making the invisible visible.
2. **Counter-facts:** Presenting a factual argument against the statement. This also relates to the microintervention strategy of educating the perpetrator.
3. **Counter-examples / Contradictions**: We combined the counterspeech strategy of pointing out contradictions with the psychology method of counter-examples.
4. **Humour:** Using humour to diffuse the situation or point out the absurdity of the claim.
5. **Warning of consequences:** Explaining the negative consequences, to the speaker or others, of making a stereotypical statement.
6. **Empathy for the speaker:** Expressing empathy with the speaker's experiences and views.
7. **Critical questions:** Asking questions to encourage the speaker to examine their beliefs more critically (Chung et al., 2019).
8. **Broadening exceptions:** Providing examples of individuals from *outside* the target group who also have the stereotypical trait (Allaway et al., 2022).
9. **Broadening universals:** Stating that all people can have the stereotypical trait, regardless of group membership (Allaway et al., 2022).
10. **Emphasizing positive qualities:** Stating positive qualities of the target group (Fraser et al., 2021).
11. **Perspective-taking:** Asking the speaker to consider how they would feel if they were part of the target group (Todd et al., 2011).

3.2 Stereotype Categories

It has been suggested that different kinds of stereotypes may be most effectively countered in different ways (FitzGerald et al., 2019; Mathew et al., 2019). Here, we focused on the following aspects:

Descriptive versus prescriptive: Descriptive stereotypes make claims about how groups *are*; prescriptive stereotypes make claims about how groups *should be*. While prescriptive stereotypes can in theory apply to any group, most of the research has focused on gender stereotypes (Prentice and Carranza, 2002; Ellemers, 2018), for example, *Boys shouldn't cry* and *Girls should be nice*.

Positive versus negative: Stereotypes are often viewed as primarily *negative*; that is, ascribing to groups traits that are not valued in society. However, stereotypes involving *positive* traits also exist (e.g., *Black people are athletic*, *Asian kids are good at math*) and have been shown to be harmful in a

Negative	Rich people are greedy.
	Native Americans are alcoholics.
	Christians are intolerant.
Positive	Gay men are fashionable.
	Asian students are good at math.
	Jewish people are wealthy.
Descriptive	Women are natural caretakers.
	Men are aggressive.
	Canadians are polite.
Prescriptive	Men should never cry.
	Women should be nice.
	Poor people should work harder.
More Accurate	Swedish people are blonde.
	Men are stronger than women.
	Muslim women wear hijab.
Inaccurate	Black people are less intelligent.
	Homeless people are dangerous.
	Muslims are terrorists.

Table 1: Example stereotypes used in this paper. In addition to the three dimensions, we attempted to cover a range of target groups, loosely categorized into the following: Purple: gender/sexuality, Red: race/nationality, Blue: socioeconomic status, Green: religion.

number of ways, including contributing to systemic inequalities (Czopp et al., 2015).

Statistically accurate versus inaccurate: While it is never true that all members of a group share all traits, some stereotypes are rooted in truth while others are completely inaccurate (Jussim et al., 2009). For example, the stereotype *Men make more money than women* is statistically accurate in most countries when considering the mean wages of men and women.[1] However, the stereotype *Muslims are terrorists* is simply incorrect and cannot be supported by any statistical argument.

For each category, we compiled several examples from the literature and popular press, aiming in the process to cover a range of different target groups. Of course, some stereotypes belong to more than one category (for the complete categorization see Appendix A). The resulting set of stereotypes in this study is given in Table 1.

3.3 Generating Counter-Stereotypes

Since our goal is to evaluate automatic means of generating counter-stereotypes, we employed a state-of-the-art generative language model ChatGPT.[2] For each counter-stereotype strategy listed in Sec. 3.1, we prompted ChatGPT with a template request in the form "`Counter the stereotype '<stereotype>' by <using strategy>. Limit your response to one sentence. Use tweet style.`" The placeholder `<using strategy>` was replaced with a phrase corresponding to a given strategy, for example, "presenting statistical counter-facts" or "broadening the statement to include other groups that have this trait". We experimented with different wordings for each strategy on a small validation set of stereotypes, and chose the prompts that resulted in responses that most closely matched the requested strategy. The full list of the final prompts is provided in Appendix B. We asked ChatGPT to limit its response to one sentence since by default it tends to generate a full paragraph and employ more than one strategy. Further, we requested the generated responses to match the style of tweets, which is less formal and more engaging for the reader. For each strategy, we produced a prompt corresponding to each of the 18 stereotypes listed in Table 1 (198 prompts in total).

3.4 Evaluation

The ChatGPT–generated responses were then manually evaluated by four annotators (the authors of the paper) for quality and expected effectiveness.[3] Prior to the annotation, the authors analyzed the generated counter-stereotypes for a set of example stereotypes in the validation set and developed the annotation guidelines (available in the Supplementary Material). The annotation consisted of two parts. In the first part, there were three questions that evaluated the quality of the ChatGPT–generated texts:

1. Does ChatGPT use the requested strategy?
2. Is the counter-stereotype offensive? That is, is it likely to cause offence to some person or group of people?
3. Is the counter-stereotype believable? Or does it seem bogus or false?

In Q3, we assessed how believable (instead of how truthful) the generated statements were since

[1] `https://www.pewresearch.org/fact-tank/2023/03/01/gender-pay-gap-facts/`

[2] We used the *OpenAI Python library* (`https://github.com/openai/openai-python`) to access the *ChatCompletion* functionality of the *gpt-3.5-turbo* (`https://platform.openai.com/docs/models/gpt-3-5`) model through its API. The temperature parameter was set to the default value of 0.7, balancing creativity and coherence of its output.

[3] All four annotators identify as women, have post-secondary education degrees, and work as researchers. They come from different cultural and religious backgrounds.

verifying the truthfulness of a statement is time-consuming and sometimes infeasible (due to the limited information provided). Moreover, we anticipate that most users would not check the presented facts.

All four annotators were in full agreement on 80% of generated texts for Q1 and on over 95% of texts for Q2 and Q3 (Fleiss' κ: 0.50 for Q1, 0.51 for Q2, and 0.39 for Q3). After each individual evaluation was completed, the four annotators discussed the cases where they disagreed and a consensus was reached for such cases. Only texts that were judged as matching the strategy, inoffensive, and believable were further annotated in part two.

In the second part, the annotators were asked if the counter-stereotype is likely to be an effective response to the corresponding stereotype. Here, our goal was to evaluate which strategy is most likely to be effective at countering stereotypes on social media. Since we assumed most annotators did not hold these stereotypes, we did not attempt to evaluate which counter-stereotypes would be most effective at changing the mind of the original speaker. Rather, we asked the annotators to consider the view of a "bystander" who happens upon the stereotype and the response on social media. The possible answers were:

- This is one of the best possible responses to this stereotype (score of 1)
- This is an OK response, but it could be better (score of 0)
- This is not a good response to this stereotype (score of -1)

This part of the evaluation was the most subjective, and we considered the answers from all four annotators by averaging the scores (rather than selecting the majority score). There was also an optional free–text response associated with this question where the annotators could explain why the strategy was particularly good or particularly bad. We use these comments to get further insights into the advantages and disadvantages of using the strategies (Sec. 4.2).

4 Results

4.1 Part 1: Evaluating ChatGPT

Figure 1 shows the results of our evaluation of ChatGPT. Some strategies were evidently more difficult to generate; in particular, *broadening exceptions* were incorrectly generated over 70% of the time. Broadening exceptions should provide examples of individuals or groups from outside the target group who have the stereotyped trait. For example, for the stereotype *Rich people are greedy*, a broadening exception could be a person who is known to be both greedy and poor. Since such examples are difficult to produce, ChatGPT often substituted a broadening universal instead, such as *Greed is not exclusive to the rich, individuals of all socioeconomic statuses can exhibit selfish and excessive behavior.* To a lesser extent, ChatGPT sometimes used the incorrect strategy when prompted for counter-examples, counter-facts, and broadening universals.

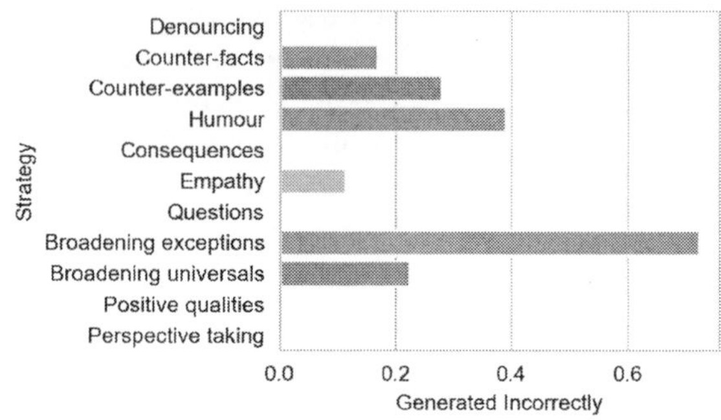

Figure 1: Proportion of times that ChatGPT generated a response that either did not use the requested strategy, was offensive, or was not believable.

We observe that ChatGPT also struggles with producing humorous responses. At this stage, annotators were instructed not to judge whether the response was truly funny or not, and so most responses were judged as having used the correct strategy. However, over a third of the humorous responses were deemed to be potentially offensive. Although humour has been identified as a useful strategy in general, the potential dangers of *automatically* generated responses using this strategy seem to outweigh the benefits. The only responses to be annotated as offensive appeared for the humour strategy.

Most of the responses generated by ChatGPT were judged as "believable," with the exception of the counter-fact *Women are less likely to provide unpaid care to family members than men.* However, see Section 5 for an assessment of how many of the generated facts are actually true.

4.2 Part 2: Evaluating Counter-Stereotype Effectiveness

Figure 2 shows the results of our evaluation of counter-stereotype effectiveness, averaged over all the stereotypes in Table 1. Overall, the annotators preferred the strategies that involved warning of consequences, empathy, and denouncing stereotypes. Some examples of these strategies include:

- **Consequences:** *Spreading the stereotype that homeless people are dangerous can further marginalize and harm those experiencing homelessness, perpetuate prejudice, and hinder efforts to provide effective solutions to the issue.*
- **Empathy:** *I understand the belief that men are stronger than women, but it's important to recognize that strength comes in many forms and should not be limited by gender. #breakingstereotypes*
- **Denouncing:** *#StopRacism: Claiming that Black people are less intelligent is an outdated and baseless stereotype that has been repeatedly debunked by research.*

Annotators observed in their discussion that "empathy" did not typically stand on its own as a strategy, but was used in conjunction with another strategy (here, a broadening universal). The strategy of denouncing was effective because it "names and shames" the statement for what it is: a stereotype, in some cases rooted in racism, sexism, or other forms of discrimination. Since most people do not think of themselves as being racist, sexist, and so on, this can be an effective deterrent. Warning of consequences can be effective because it goes beyond denouncing to explain the real-world impact of the stereotype on the target group.

In general, counter-examples and humour were rated as less convincing strategies. Annotators often commented that the "jokes" generated by ChatGPT were not funny or did not make sense. The counter-examples were ineffective for a different reason, namely that the existence of one or two individuals who did not fit the stereotype is not convincing evidence that the stereotype does not hold true in general (i.e., they were seen as "the exception that proves the rule").

The strategies of providing counter-facts, asking questions, stating broadening universals, and promoting perspective-taking were seen as weakly positive. Broadening universals were sometimes seen as too generic, and the questions sometimes didn't make sense or could be answered in a way that actually confirmed the stereotype. Broadening exceptions (when they were generated correctly) and emphasizing positive qualities were rated as weakly negative. In particular, annotator comments indicated that positive qualities were often unrelated to the stereotype, or did not necessarily counter/contradict the stereotype (e.g., *Muslim women are educated, strong, resilient, kindhearted, and have diverse talents and interests* says nothing about whether Muslim women wear hijab).

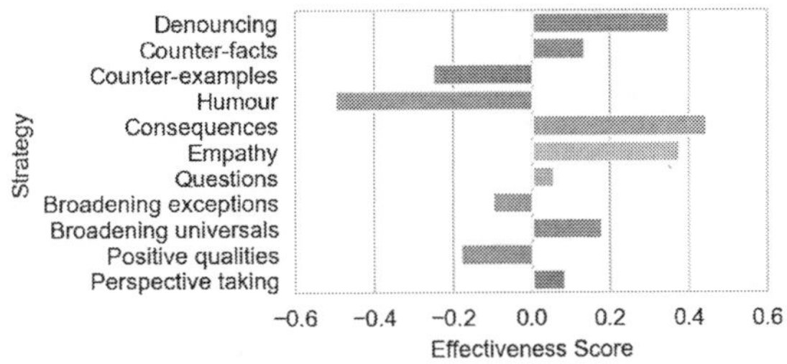

Figure 2: Overall evaluation of counter-stereotype effectiveness, with +1 corresponding to *This is one of the best possible responses to this stereotype* and -1 corresponding to *This is not a good response to this stereotype.*

Although some overall trends are clear, we also hypothesize that certain strategies may be more effective depending on the situation. Figure 3 shows the results of our evaluation of counter-stereotype effectiveness, broken down along the three dimensions previously identified.

When contrasting so-called "positive" and "negative" stereotypes, a few observations jump out. Broadening exceptions are much less effective for negative stereotypes than in the overall case, likely because they ascribe negative traits to other social groups, which can sound rude—e.g., *Stereotyping Native Americans as alcoholics is unfair and inaccurate, as many other ethnic and cultural groups also struggle with alcoholism.* We also see that empathy was rated higher for positive stereotypes than negative stereotypes, as empathizing with highly negative viewpoints was not seen as appropriate.

A number of salient differences were seen when countering prescriptive versus descriptive stereotypes. The strategies of denouncing, consequences, empathy, critical questions, and broadening universals were more highly rated for countering prescriptive stereotypes. In particular, while asking critical questions was rated neutrally overall (Figure 2), it was judged to be an effective strategy for prescriptive stereotypes. An example of this is: *Why should women constantly prioritize being "nice" over advocating for themselves and standing up for what they believe in? #BreakTheStereotype* Annotators also commented on the difficulty of providing counter-examples and counter-facts to

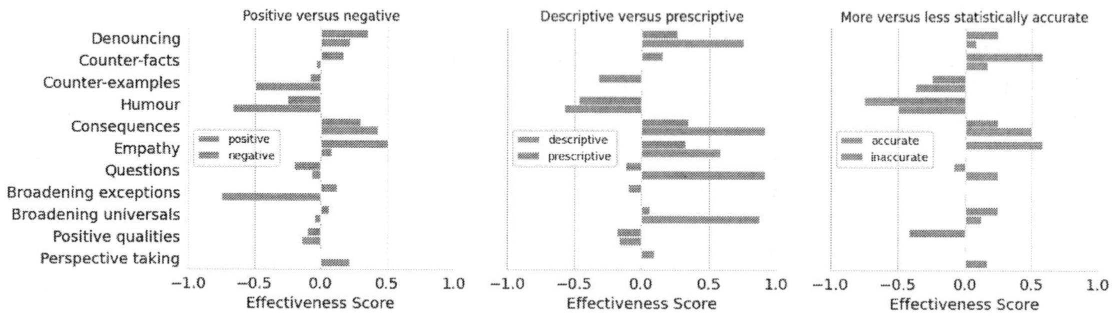

Figure 3: The effectiveness of the strategies for different types of stereotypes.

prescriptive stereotypes. For example, the counter-fact *Contrary to popular belief, men do cry - on average, men cry between 6 and 17 times per year* was seen by some annotators as ineffective, because arguing that men *do* cry is not the same as saying men *should* cry.

Finally, we contrast the results for stereotypes that are more statistically accurate versus those that are highly statistically inaccurate. Somewhat counter-intuitively, counter-facts were rated as *more* effective when the stereotype had more basis in reality. In particular, one response was rated as extremely poor: *Less than 0.1% of Muslims have been involved in terrorism-related activities, according to a study by the University of North Carolina. #NotAllMuslims #StopIslamophobia.* This "fact" had passed the filtering phase for believability due to the phrase "less than," but annotators were concerned that it vastly over-stated the percentage of Muslims involved in terrorism. This underscores the importance of providing accurate facts. If ChatGPT cannot generate reliable statistics, it may be more effective to stick with general statements.

5 Discussion

From the results presented in the previous section, we discuss some high-level observations.

Counter-stereotypes should not be offensive. In generating counter-stereotypes, we do not want to offend the speaker, the target group, or perpetuate new and harmful stereotypes. None of the content generated by ChatGPT was overtly obscene or hateful. However, some of the "humourous" responses were flagged as having the potential to offend. In particular, the appropriateness of ChatGPT—a disembodied machine learning algorithm—claiming various cultural identities was seen as problematic, as in the following: *Just because I'm Native American doesn't mean I have a drinking problem, I just have a healthy appreciation for fermented berries. #NotAllNativesAreAlcoholics.* In general, we believe that ChatGPT should not claim membership in any human social groups.

Counter-stereotypes should not spread misinformation. In our evaluation of ChatGPT (Section 4.1), each statement was annotated as "believable or bogus", with the idea that being believable is a prerequisite to being an effective counter-stereotype. Actually fact-checking the counter-examples and counter-facts is not straightforward, as statements like "9.3% of Jewish households live in poverty" could be true or false in different contexts (geographic location, year, definition of poverty, etc.). Furthermore, one limitation of ChatGPT is that it rarely cites sources for its facts. However, we did fact-check the counter-examples and counter-statements to the best of our ability, and found that approximately 40% of the facts presented were either incorrect or could not be verified. Even if these statements are believable and could be effective in changing people's minds, it would not be appropriate to use them if they are not accurate.

Combining strategies may be most effective. We observe that ChatGPT often combines strategies to some extent. For example, a counter-stereotype might use an empathetic tone, provide a counter-fact, and denounce stereotyping. We believe this could be further developed by explicitly prompting ChatGPT to use multiple strategies simultaneously. Similarly, strategies which were less effective on their own (such as broadening universals, which act more to challenge the idea that social groups are meaningful categorizations than to specifically counter the given stereotype) might be more effective when used in combination with more direct strategies.

6 Conclusion

This study represents a preliminary pilot study, with the aim of narrowing down the set of strategies to test in a subsequent user study. Therefore, our goal is not to determine which strategy is the most effective, but rather to define a small set of most promising strategies for further investigation.

Our analysis indicates that while ChatGPT can generate remarkably appropriate and believable responses using most of the strategies, there are certain pitfalls that must be avoided. For the reasons discussed, we do not recommend using ChatGPT to automatically generate counter-stereotypes using the strategies of humour, counter-facts, counter-examples, or broadening exceptions. Furthermore, the annotators did not rate the strategies of broadening universals or emphasizing positive qualities as particularly effective.

Three strategies emerged as being promising candidates in many circumstances: denouncing, warning of consequences, and using an empathetic tone. Empathetic tone can be combined with other strategies to increase the civility of the response; however, bystanders might be offended if the response is *too* empathetic to highly offensive views.

The remaining strategies of asking critical questions and promoting perspective-taking require further study. Critical questions were rated as particularly effective in the case of prescriptive stereotypes, which are harder to counter with facts, as they represent beliefs about how the world *should* be rather than how it *is*. Probing the speaker to re-examine why they hold these beliefs may be more successful in this case. Perspective-taking also turns the focus inwards, asking things like *How would you feel if someone said that about your group?* and while the annotators did not find this strategy convincing from the bystander perspective, it may be useful for individuals who actually hold the stereotypical belief.

Limitations

In this preliminary study we assumed that a stereotype is expressed explicitly in a conversation. Yet, in real-life communications this may not be the case as stereotypical views can be expressed in implicit and subtle ways. Unraveling the implicit meaning of a message can be challenging for AI and humans and may require specific background knowledge or experience.

The current study evaluated counter-stereotypes for 18 common North American stereotypes categorized for three aspects: descriptive/prescriptive, positive/negative, and statistically accurate/inaccurate. Psychological theories of stereotype content further divide stereotypes along various dimensions, like warmth and competence (Fiske et al., 2007), or agency, beliefs, and communion (Koch et al., 2016). While the aspect of positivity/negativity of a stereotype partially captures these dimensions, further studies need to examine the effectiveness of the counter-stereotype strategies for ambivalent stereotypes (i.e., positive on one dimension, but negative on the other(s)).

The ChatGPT–generated texts were affected by the chosen phrasing of the prompts. Further, as a generative language model, ChatGPT is designed to generate varying outputs even for the same prompt. In our validation phase, we observed that for some strategies the content of the responses varied only slightly across different runs, while for strategies requiring more creative output (e.g., humour, critical questions) the responses could diverge substantially. Future work should assess the stability of the responses for various strategies and the accuracy and effectiveness of the responses generated with varying temperature parameters of ChatGPT, as well as exploring other generative large language models.

In this study, our goal was to evaluate the suitability of the current state-of-the-art NLP technology for generating counter-stereotypes and to obtain some insights into which strategies can be effective in social media conversations. However, our group of annotators was small and not representative of society in general. As individual users can be affected differently by various countering strategies, depending on their backgrounds and lived experiences, a further evaluation of the potential effectiveness of the strategies with a broader pool of users would be valuable. Also, as we discussed above, combining various strategies in one response is a promising way forward and needs further investigation.

Ethics Statement

Countering stereotypical views and statements can have a tremendous positive effect on making online spaces more inclusive and safe for everyone and reducing prejudice and discrimination. However, certain responses can do more harm than good. Addressing stereotypical views in a hostile or offensive way only fuels the conflict. Producing and perpetuating new stereotypes while denouncing the old ones may create a vicious cycle. To reduce the possible negative effects, care should be exercised in which automatic techniques to use and how to deploy them in real-life applications. Wherever possible, an AI-in-the-loop paradigm should be employed where users are assisted by the technology, but remain in control.

Acknowledgements

Anna Kerkhof acknowledges funding by the Bavarian State Ministry of Science and the Arts in the framework of the bidt Graduate Center for Postdocs.

References

Emily Allaway, Nina Taneja, Sarah-Jane Leslie, and Maarten Sap. 2022. Towards countering essentialism through social bias reasoning. In *Poster, Workshop on NLP for Positive Impact*.

Mana Ashida and Mamoru Komachi. 2022. Towards automatic generation of messages countering online hate speech and microaggressions. In *Proceedings of the Sixth Workshop on Online Abuse and Harms (WOAH)*, pages 11–23, Seattle, Washington (Hybrid). Association for Computational Linguistics.

Susan Benesch, Derek Ruths, Kelly P Dillon, Haji Mohammad Saleem, and Lucas Wright. 2016a. *Considerations for successful counterspeech*. Dangerous Speech Project.

Susan Benesch, Derek Ruths, Kelly P Dillon, Haji Mohammad Saleem, and Lucas Wright. 2016b. *Counterspeech on Twitter: A field study*. Dangerous Speech Project.

Sarai Blincoe and Monica J Harris. 2009. Prejudice reduction in white students: Comparing three conceptual approaches. *Journal of Diversity in Higher Education*, 2(4):232.

Tolga Bolukbasi, Kai-Wei Chang, James Y Zou, Venkatesh Saligrama, and Adam T Kalai. 2016. Man is to computer programmer as woman is to homemaker? debiasing word embeddings. In *Advances in Neural Information Processing Systems*, pages 4349–4357.

Helena Bonaldi, Sara Dellantonio, Serra Sinem Tekiroğlu, and Marco Guerini. 2022. Human-machine collaboration approaches to build a dialogue dataset for hate speech countering. In *Proceedings of the 2022 Conference on Empirical Methods in Natural Language Processing*, pages 8031–8049, Abu Dhabi, United Arab Emirates. Association for Computational Linguistics.

Aylin Caliskan, Joanna J Bryson, and Arvind Narayanan. 2017. Semantics derived automatically from language corpora contain human-like biases. *Science*, 356(6334):183–186.

Tessa ES Charlesworth, Victor Yang, Thomas C Mann, Benedek Kurdi, and Mahzarin R Banaji. 2021. Gender stereotypes in natural language: Word embeddings show robust consistency across child and adult language corpora of more than 65 million words. *Psychological Science*, 32(2):218–240.

Yi-Ling Chung, Elizaveta Kuzmenko, Serra Sinem Tekiroglu, and Marco Guerini. 2019. CONAN - COunter NArratives through nichesourcing: a multilingual dataset of responses to fight online hate speech. In *Proceedings of the 57th Annual Meeting of the Association for Computational Linguistics*, pages 2819–2829, Florence, Italy. Association for Computational Linguistics.

Alexander M Czopp, Aaron C Kay, and Sapna Cheryan. 2015. Positive stereotypes are pervasive and powerful. *Perspectives on Psychological Science*, 10(4):451–463.

Nilanjana Dasgupta and Anthony G Greenwald. 2001. On the malleability of automatic attitudes: combating automatic prejudice with images of admired and disliked individuals. *Journal of Personality and Social Psychology*, 81(5):800.

Naomi Ellemers. 2018. Gender stereotypes. *Annual Review of Psychology*, 69:275–298.

Margherita Fanton, Helena Bonaldi, Serra Sinem Tekiroğlu, and Marco Guerini. 2021. Human-in-the-loop for data collection: a multi-target counter narrative dataset to fight online hate speech. In *Proceedings of the 59th Annual Meeting of the Association for Computational Linguistics and the 11th International Joint Conference on Natural Language Processing (Volume 1: Long Papers)*, pages 3226–3240, Online. Association for Computational Linguistics.

Susan T Fiske, Amy JC Cuddy, and Peter Glick. 2007. Universal dimensions of social cognition: Warmth and competence. *Trends in Cognitive Sciences*, 11(2):77–83.

Chloë FitzGerald, Angela Martin, Delphine Berner, and Samia Hurst. 2019. Interventions designed to reduce implicit prejudices and implicit stereotypes in real world contexts: a systematic review. *BMC Psychology*, 7(1):1–12.

Antske Fokkens, Nel Ruigrok, Camiel Beukeboom, Gagestein Sarah, and Wouter Van Atteveldt. 2018. Studying Muslim stereotyping through microportrait extraction. In *Proceedings of the Eleventh International Conference on Language Resources and Evaluation (LREC 2018)*.

Patrick S Forscher, Calvin K Lai, Jordan R Axt, Charles R Ebersole, Michelle Herman, Patricia G Devine, and Brian A Nosek. 2019. A meta-analysis of procedures to change implicit measures. *Journal of Personality and Social Psychology*, 117(3):522.

Kathleen C. Fraser, Isar Nejadgholi, and Svetlana Kiritchenko. 2021. Understanding and countering stereotypes: A computational approach to the stereotype content model. In *Proceedings of the 59th Annual Meeting of the Association for Computational Linguistics and the 11th International Joint Conference on Natural Language Processing (Volume 1: Long Papers)*, pages 600–616, Online. Association for Computational Linguistics.

Nikhil Garg, Londa Schiebinger, Dan Jurafsky, and James Zou. 2018. Word embeddings quantify 100 years of gender and ethnic stereotypes. *Proceedings of the National Academy of Sciences*, 115(16):E3635–E3644.

Anthony G Greenwald, Debbie E McGhee, and Jordan LK Schwartz. 1998. Measuring individual differences in implicit cognition: the implicit association test. *Journal of Personality and Social Psychology*, 74(6):1464.

Lee Jussim, Thomas R Cain, Jarret T Crawford, Kent Harber, and Florette Cohen. 2009. The unbearable accuracy of stereotypes. *Handbook of prejudice, stereotyping, and discrimination*, 199:227.

Alex Koch, Roland Imhoff, Ron Dotsch, Christian Unkelbach, and Hans Alves. 2016. The ABC of stereotypes about groups: Agency/socioeconomic success, conservative–progressive beliefs, and communion. *Journal of Personality and Social Psychology*, 110(5):675.

Ben Krause, Akhilesh Deepak Gotmare, Bryan McCann, Nitish Shirish Keskar, Shafiq Joty, Richard Socher, and Nazneen Fatema Rajani. 2021. GeDi: Generative discriminator guided sequence generation. In *Findings of the Association for Computational Linguistics: EMNLP 2021*, pages 4929–4952, Punta Cana, Dominican Republic. Association for Computational Linguistics.

Yousri Marzouki, Eliza Barach, Vidhushini Srinivasan, Samira Shaikh, and Laurie Beth Feldman. 2020. The dynamics of negative stereotypes as revealed by tweeting behavior in the aftermath of the Charlie Hebdo terrorist attack. *Heliyon*, 6(8):e04311.

Binny Mathew, Punyajoy Saha, Hardik Tharad, Subham Rajgaria, Prajwal Singhania, Suman Kalyan Maity, Pawan Goyal, and Animesh Mukherjee. 2019. Thou shalt not hate: Countering online hate speech. In *Proceedings of the International AAAI Conference on Web and Social Media*, volume 13, pages 369–380.

Jozef Miškolci, Lucia Kováčová, and Edita Rigová. 2020. Countering hate speech on Facebook: The case of the Roma minority in Slovakia. *Social Science Computer Review*, 38(2):128–146.

Moin Nadeem, Anna Bethke, and Siva Reddy. 2021. StereoSet: Measuring stereotypical bias in pretrained language models. In *Proceedings of the 59th Annual Meeting of the Association for Computational Linguistics and the 11th International Joint Conference on Natural Language Processing (Volume 1: Long Papers)*, pages 5356–5371, Online. Association for Computational Linguistics.

Tabitha C Peck, Sofia Seinfeld, Salvatore M Aglioti, and Mel Slater. 2013. Putting yourself in the skin of a black avatar reduces implicit racial bias. *Consciousness and Cognition*, 22(3):779–787.

Deborah A Prentice and Erica Carranza. 2002. What women and men should be, shouldn't be, are allowed to be, and don't have to be: The contents of prescriptive gender stereotypes. *Psychology of Women Quarterly*, 26(4):269–281.

Jing Qian, Anna Bethke, Yinyin Liu, Elizabeth Belding, and William Yang Wang. 2019. A benchmark dataset for learning to intervene in online hate speech. In *Proceedings of the 2019 Conference on Empirical Methods in Natural Language Processing and the 9th International Joint Conference on Natural Language Processing (EMNLP-IJCNLP)*, pages 4755–4764, Hong Kong, China. Association for Computational Linguistics.

Punyajoy Saha, Kanishk Singh, Adarsh Kumar, Binny Mathew, and Animesh Mukherjee. 2022. CounterGeDi: A controllable approach to generate polite, detoxified and emotional counterspeech. In *Proceedings of the Thirty-First International Joint Conference on Artificial Intelligence, IJCAI-22*, pages 5157–5163. International Joint Conferences on Artificial Intelligence Organization. AI for Good.

Claude M Steele. 2011. *Whistling Vivaldi: How stereotypes affect us and what we can do.* WW Norton & Company.

Derald Wing Sue, Sarah Alsaidi, Michael N Awad, Elizabeth Glaeser, Cassandra Z Calle, and Narolyn Mendez. 2019. Disarming racial microaggressions: Microintervention strategies for targets, white allies, and bystanders. *American Psychologist*, 74(1):128.

Andrew R Todd, Galen V Bodenhausen, Jennifer A Richeson, and Adam D Galinsky. 2011. Perspective taking combats automatic expressions of racial bias. *Journal of Personality and Social Psychology*, 100(6):1027.

Natalie A Wyer. 2010. Salient egalitarian norms moderate activation of out-group approach and avoidance. *Group Processes & Intergroup Relations*, 13(2):151–165.

Wanzheng Zhu and Suma Bhat. 2021. Generate, prune, select: A pipeline for counterspeech generation against online hate speech. In *Findings of the Association for Computational Linguistics: ACL-IJCNLP 2021*, pages 134–149, Online. Association for Computational Linguistics.

A Stereotype Categories

Table A.1 lists all 18 selected stereotypes and their categorization along the three dimensions: descriptive vs. prescriptive, positive vs. negative, statistically accurate vs. inaccurate. Most of the stereotypes are descriptive and negative. Prescriptive stereotypes tend to be used to describe the expected roles and behaviours for girls/women and boys/men in society. Since prescriptive stereotypes state how the world *should be*, the stereotypes are neither positive nor negative, neither accurate nor inaccurate. Descriptive stereotypes can be more or less statistically accurate, but it is often hard to estimate their exact accuracy since the information may not be available and/or varies across regions and times. For this study, we selected three stereotypes with high statistical accuracy and three stereotypes with very low statistical accuracy. The categorization reported in this table is used in Sec. 4.2 for calculating the evaluation scores of counter-stereotype effectiveness broken down along the three dimensions (Fig. 3).

B Counter-Stereotype Prompts

Table B.1 lists the final prompts used for each counter-stereotype strategy and gives examples of texts generated by ChatGPT in response to these prompts.

Stereotype	Descriptive/Prescriptive	Positive/Negative	Accurate/Inaccurate
Rich people are greedy.	descriptive	negative	
Native Americans are alcoholics.	descriptive	negative	
Christians are intolerant.	descriptive	negative	
Gay men are fashionable.	descriptive	positive	
Asian students are good at math.	descriptive	positive	
Jewish people are wealthy.	descriptive	positive	
Women are natural caretakers.	descriptive	positive	
Men are aggressive.	descriptive	negative	
Canadians are polite.	descriptive	positive	
Men should never cry.	prescriptive		
Women should be nice.	prescriptive		
Poor people should work harder.	prescriptive		
Swedish people are blonde.	descriptive		accurate
Men are stronger than women.	descriptive		accurate
Muslim women wear hijab.	descriptive		accurate
Black people are less intelligent.	descriptive	negative	inaccurate
Homeless people are dangerous.	descriptive	negative	inaccurate
Muslims are terrorists.	descriptive	negative	inaccurate

Table A.1: The 18 selected stereotypes categorized along the three dimensions: descriptive vs. prescriptive, positive vs. negative, statistically accurate vs. inaccurate.

Counter Strategy	Prompt	ChatGPT–Generated Text
Denouncement of stereotypes	Denounce the statement '<stereotype>' as a stereotype. Limit your response to one sentence. Use tweet style.	Women are not born with a natural inclination towards caregiving, the gendered societal roles assigned to them only perpetuate this harmful stereotype. #EndGender-Stereotypes
Counter-facts	Counter the stereotype '<stereotype>' by presenting statistical counter-facts. Limit your response to one sentence. Use tweet style.	Women are less likely to provide unpaid care to family members than men, with 27% of women providing care compared to 31% of men. #genderdata #caregiving (Implausible)
Counter-examples / Contradictions	Counter the stereotype '<stereotype>' with examples of real people. Limit your response to one sentence. Use tweet style.	"Dr. Jane Goodall, a world-renowned primatologist, has devoted her life to studying and protecting chimpanzees and their habitats." #WomenBreakingBarriers (Incorrect strategy: does not counter the stereotype)
Humour	Counter the stereotype '<stereotype>' by using humor. Limit your response to one sentence. Use tweet style.	"Women may be natural caretakers, but have you seen us try to assemble IKEA furniture?" #justcalltheguy (Potentially offensive)
Warning of consequences	Counter the stereotype '<stereotype>' by warning of the consequences of spreading this stereotype. Limit your response to one sentence. Use tweet style.	Spreading the stereotype that women are natural caretakers reinforces gender roles and can lead to women being expected to take on any care-related tasks, regardless of whether they want to or have the capacity to do so.
Empathy for the speaker	Counter the stereotype '<stereotype>' by expressing empathy to the people believing in this. Limit your response to one sentence. Use tweet style.	I understand why some people may believe that women are natural caretakers, but gender does not determine one's ability or inclination to provide care. #EndGender-Stereotypes
Critical questions	Counter the stereotype '<stereotype>' with a thought-provoking question to the reader. Limit your response to one sentence. Use tweet style.	What about women who don't want to be caretakers, and men who do? #breakthestereotype
Broadening exceptions	Counter the stereotype '<stereotype>' by broadening the statement to include other groups that have this trait. Limit your response to one sentence. Use tweet style.	"Individuals who possess a nurturing personality regardless of gender should be acknowledged as natural caretakers." #genderneutral #nurturingtrait (Incorrect strategy: used Broadening Universals)
Broadening universals	Counter the stereotype '<stereotype>' by broadening the statement to include all people that have this trait. Limit your response to one sentence. Use tweet style.	"People with a strong caretaking trait are valuable members of society, regardless of gender." #breakstereotypes
Emphasizing positive qualities	Counter the stereotype '<stereotype>' by listing positive characteristics of the group. Limit your response to one sentence. Use tweet style.	Women are natural leaders, problem-solvers, and innovators, capable of achieving any goal! #ShatterTheStereotype
Perspective-taking	Counter the stereotype '<stereotype>' by asking the speaker to consider how they would feel if they were part of the target group. Limit your response to one sentence. Use tweet style.	Would you like to be pigeonholed into a role based on your gender? #NoToStereotypes #EqualOpportunities

Table B.1: Prompts used for each counter-stereotype strategy and example texts generated by ChatGPT for stereotype *"Women are natural caretakers"*. Texts in red were identified by the annotators as unsuitable due to the incorrect strategy, potential offensiveness, or implausibility.

BCause: Reducing group bias and promoting cohesive discussion in online deliberation processes through a simple and engaging online deliberation tool

Lucas Anastasiou and **Anna De Liddo**
Knowledge Media Institute
The Open University
United Kingdom

Abstract

Facilitating healthy online deliberation in terms of sensemaking and collaboration of discussion participants proves extremely challenging due to a number of known negative effects of online communication on social media platforms. We start from concerns and aspirations about the use of existing online discussion systems as distilled in previous literature, we then combine them with lessons learned on design and engineering practices from our research team, to inform the design of an easy-to-use tool (BCause.app) that enables higher quality discussions than traditional social media. We describe the design of this tool, highlighting the main interaction features that distinguish it from common social media, namely: i. the low-cost argumentation structuring of the conversations with direct replies; ii. and the distinctive use of reflective feedback rather than appreciative-only feedback. We then present the results of a controlled A/B experiment in which we show that the presence of argumentative and cognitive reflective discussion elements produces better social interaction with less polarization and promotes a more cohesive discussion than common social media-like interactions.

1 Introduction

Deliberation is the process of careful discussion before decision, and it can be defined as the thorough dialogical assessment of the reasons for and against a measure before a decision is made. When teams are geographically distributed, decision making is made more difficult by the fact that these thorough conversations cannot happen face-to-face, with people sitting in the same room. Deliberation is therefore carried out online, with social media and online discussion technologies, that are generally limited in features, are not designed to support decision making, and often produce polarisation, division and conflict (Sunstein, 2018; Golbeck et al., 2017; Matias et al., 2015; Binder et al., 2009). This is due to a series of well-known negative effects of online communication on social media discussion platforms such as the "echo chamber" effect and the activation of biased information dynamics (Ditto and Lopez, 1992; Taber and Lodge, 2006). Research evidence clearly indicates that people tend to select information from people who hold similar positions and support similar worldviews (Huckfeldt and Sprague, 1995; Mutz, 2001). On this account, social media companies, that seek consumers satisfaction in the first place, have designed social media platforms to recommend content on the base of similarity, popularity and agreement-only principles (France, 2017). This implies that diversity of opinions and disagreement is "by design" less likely to be found in the same social media endeavour, creating platform islands, group think and isolation effects. This combination of homophily and lack of content variety has proved to degrade the quality, balance and safety (Golbeck et al., 2017; Guntuku et al., 2017) of online discourse, up to undermining social tolerance (Mutz, 2002).

In this paper, we describe the initial design and evaluation of a new platform for online deliberation BCause[1], designed to be highly usable yet enable higher quality discussions than traditional social media. We present a user study and A/B tests that show how BCause improves engagement and collaboration while reducing group bias in online discussions.

2 Background knowledge

Online deliberation focuses on the challenge of sustaining discourse and collaborative knowledge construction through crowdsourcing unstructured contributions to online dialogue. As a field of research, it plays a crucial role in understanding and implementing new deliberative citizenship prac-

[1] http://bcause.app

Proceedings of the First Workshop on Social Influence in Conversations (SICon 2023), pages 39–49

tices (Law and Urry, 2004). In its most empowering interpretations, online deliberation research and practice should be intrinsically driven by the effort to produce democratically reflective citizens and to "align with the less powerful rather than reproduce the power of the already dominant" (Coleman and Moss, 2012). Research on online deliberation is thus strongly linked to democratic values and aspirations and focuses on a bottom-up view of responsible citizenship and civic behavior (Barnett, 2003; Dean, 1999). A comprehensive review of the literature on online deliberation found that despite the diversity of definitions and applications of the term, there are six main operating principles that should guide the theory and applications of online deliberation: rationality, interactivity, equality, civility, concern for the common good, and constructive attitude (Friess and Eilders, 2015). Numerous technologies have been proposed in the literature to facilitate online deliberation capabilities, from social media to targeted participatory democracy solutions (such as Decidim[2], Consul[3], Loomio[4], etc.). While methods and skills to facilitate online dialogue have already been proposed in the literature (Collison et al., 2000), technologies for structured and quality online dialogue are still lacking. Personal e-mail systems, chat rooms, Twitter or Facebook conversations, as well as most interfaces for deliberative democracy solutions (as the ones mentioned above) are not much different from common discussion forums, where the thread of messages follows the temporal sequence of the dialogue, without regard to the issues raised, the structure of the discussion and the relevance of those issues in the ongoing conversation. The literature on online deliberation argues that topic and issue mapping tools (Conklin, 2008) provide better virtual environments for online discussion because they keep the focus on the issue rather than the time thread (as in normal discussion forums), thus avoiding noise and improving content understanding and navigation (Klein and Iandoli, 2008). However, these tools have so far struggled to spread, mainly due to usability issues and lack of capacity to enable more intuitive and inclusive narrative forms of dialogue and deliberation.

In general there is a plethora of shortcoming with discussion occurring online. For instance, the difficulty to ensure that all participants have an equal opportunity to contribute to the discussion.(e.g. Wikipedia edits (Shaw and Hargittai, 2018). This can be especially challenging in large group discussions, where some voices may be drowned out by others (Shortall et al., 2021). Moreover, sometimes in heated debates participants get sidetracked or engage in personal attacks. This can make it difficult for the group to reach a consensus or make a well-reasoned decision (Neurauter-Kessels, 2013). Apart of organic difficulties, online discussions can also be subject to manipulation or bias where abusers heavily dominate or direct discussion (e.g. (Elyashar et al., 2017a)), as it can be difficult to verify the identity of participants or ensure that they are acting in good faith (Elyashar et al., 2017b).

Online discussion platforms can be however a powerful tool for group deliberation, it is important though, to carefully consider these potential drawbacks when using them. Specific to this study, we attend the following issues of online discussion:

- *Polarization*: participants become more entrenched in their positions and less willing to consider other perspectives. This can happen for a variety of reasons, such as the tendency of people to seek out information that confirms their existing beliefs, or the fact that online discussions can sometimes become heated or adversarial (Boyd, 2023). This leads to more division rather than coming to a consensus. This is usually aviated by establishing ground rules (or a protocol of interaction), heavy moderation with users with aleviated rights and explicit role to to ensure that discussion remains civil and productive, or encouraging participants to consider different perspectives (Strandberg et al., 2019). But this moderation comes with high costs and often does not allow conversations to be supported at scale. Reducing polarisation in non-moderated platforms is an open challenge. Social media are indeed the predominant solution to un-moderated online discussions but have been demonstrated to contribute to increasing polarization either by amplifying or escalating social processes that also occur offline. (Iandoli et al., 2021).

- *Shallow content*: In some cases, online discussions may be quite deep and consist of well-reasoned, thought-provoking content (Hara

[2] https://decidim.org/
[3] https://consulproject.org/en/
[4] https://www.loomio.com/

et al., 2000; Gilbert and Dabbagh, 2005). In the majority of the cases though, the content may be more shallow and consist of superficial or unoriginal ideas (Maurino, 2007). Ultimately, the depth of an online discussion will depend on the quality of the participants and the effort they put into contributing to the conversation (Amichai-Hamburger et al., 2016). Regardless though, to encourage deep, meaningful discussions, it can be helpful to provide clear guidelines for participation and to encourage participants to carefully consider their ideas before posting (Zhang; Wang, 2019), this still requires human moderation of the conversation and it remains an issue in unmoderated discussion systems.

- *Sensemaking* in online discussion can prove problematic. As large discussions can be chaotic or disorganized, it is difficult for participants to follow the conversation or understand what is being discussed (Abbas et al., 2018). Additionally, not only the discussion itself but also the large number of participants, makes it challenging for individuals to keep track of all the different ideas being discussed and their provenance (who tells what). Which is setting the premise to claim that argumentative discussion could helps towards improving participants' sensemaking. Argumentation technologies have been shown to support sensemaking (Carstens et al., 2015) but lack engagement and uptake from a larger user community.

- *Collaboration*: While the promise of online discussion is a highly collaborative environment where participants are working together effectively to generate new ideas, share information, and make decisions, the reality is that is usually realised as less efficient, with participants struggling to effectively communicate and work together. Factors that can affect the quality of collaboration in online discussions (Blake and Scanlon, 2012) include the clarity of the discussion goals, the diversity of perspectives represented, and the reciprocity of communication (which enables idea refinement and common ground building).

3 Motivation

This motivates the design of a new online deliberation system which can be highly usable and equally engaging than current social media while providing structure to the online conversation so to improve the quality of sensemaking and collaboration in the online discussion process.

Our main hypothesis is that the right design decisions on the structure and functionalities would benefit the quality of the deliberation itself and the sensemaking of participants in it. Commonly used social interfaces have a great impact in people's political behaviour and decision-making in general (Lewandowsky et al., 2020) - without any design intervention they even risk aiding and abetting hateful rhetorics (Bail, 2022). Our motivation is to address the challenge for building large scale online discussion platform by exploring new user interface paradigms which combine structuring with usability thus providing powerful technologies for highly usable deliberation on the Web. To achieve this we followed an approach that combines two main innovations:

- (i) *Low cost Argumentation Structuring* with direct replies: we designed a highly usable UI for users to contribute structured arguments while maintaining the possibility to directly address participants to the discussion, by replying to their contributions as in a normal online conversation. By providing direct replies (often missing in argumentation technology) we hope to enable reciprocity and social interaction without losing focus on the issues and structure of the conversation. This tradeoff between structure and sociability aims to improve engagement with the conversation.

- (ii) *distinctive use of reflection feedback* (rather than appreciation only mechanism): to support sensemaking of participants to the discussion while reducing group think and polarisation we designed a reflection mechanism for users to focus on the key value being civic, quality democratic deliberation. Such process aims to shift participants from perceiving the debate as a winning-losing contest and focus instead on the value of collaboration, trust and evidence-based thinking.

We followed an agile development approach constituted in a series of test and learn phases in which design ideas where proposed, prototyped and quickly tested in the design team. This was consisting of two UX designers and two software engineers who specialised in argumentation technologies. In formulating our design, we drew inspiration from established argumentation technological tools; attempting to utilise their strengths and mitigate their limitations. After several test and learn cycles, which lasted one and half year, we produced the first fully functioning interface ready for testing which we describe below.

4 Design

Our approach is to design a tool that considers the impact of it on society and individuals and mitigates the problematic phenomena observed in these systems. This is in alignment with Value Sensitive Design (VSD) (Friedman et al., 2002) approach of supporting human values and promoting social justice.

Following a kickoff meeting where we used Q-Methodology adapted for HCI (O'Leary et al., 2013), we set a list of aspirations and fears of our designers and engineers. After establishing a theoretical foundation for the values and principles that would guide our platform's design, we initiated the development process, utilizing iterative design sprints (Banfield et al., 2015). A number of the design aspirations identified require systemic organizational actions. Such actions are but are not limited to, the facilitation of diverse modalities of online dialogue, such as informal and goal-oriented discussions, the integration of collective decision-making techniques within business or enterprise workflows, and the development of an agile system that can be readily adapted to meet community requirements. While those go beyond system design, other guidelines can be followed by making design choices in terms of UX/UI. For instance design processes that allow users to inspect, confirm, dispute and correct past conversations, facilitate transparency, especially in key pieces of information processes, avoid pure argument-centric solutions, employ hybrid interfaces that retain time order and loosely visualize argument structures, are some candidate solutions. This process helped to elicit users' perspectives and finally deduce the following design interventions:

- *Argument-centric structure* of discussion. We organise the deliberation as tree structure made up of debate topics (issue to be discussed), positions (opinions or possible solutions to the topic imposed), and arguments (statements that support (pro) or oppose (con) the parent position), see Figure 1 This follows the well known paradigm of IBIS system (Kunz and Rittel, 1970; Walton, 2005) and it has many advantages such as better signal-to-noise ratio, logical structure, implicit encouragement to support with hard evidence, and others, but is not widely adopted as it is considered difficult to integrate in scale and is thought to require skillful information mappers, and enables limited participation.

- *Agreement* slider: Before entering a pro or con argument, a user is asked to enter their level of support or disagreement to the given position (ranging from "Strongly disagree" to "Strongly agree", see Figure 4. This is a gentle implicit "nudge" to reflect and state their agreement before supporting/refuting it with a concrete argument. In the end, he is shown the collective distribution of the group agreements on this position.

- *Reflection* card: We identified four important reflection dimensions: *trustworthiness* (of the information given in the position), whether the position is *polarized*, whether it should be *prioritized* and prediction of the *group agreement* on it, see Figure 2. In the end, their reflection is visualised in a radial chart along with the community's average - to provoke a comparison to the "crowd" mean. Together with *agreement slider*, they are considered nuanced reflective feedback elements (not only appreciative-only as "like"/"thank you").

- *Reply* functionality: a reply button enables to directly address a position or argument - without entering an additional position, see Figure 3 This helps to incorporate additional semantic information and scope user's action context.

5 Research question

Our main hypothesis is that the right design decisions on the structure and functionalities, along with efficient incorporation of computational tools in online deliberation platforms would benefit the quality of the deliberation itself and the sensemaking of participants in it. Our motivation is to address the challenge for building large scale online discussion platform while balancing a critical tension between providing advanced computational

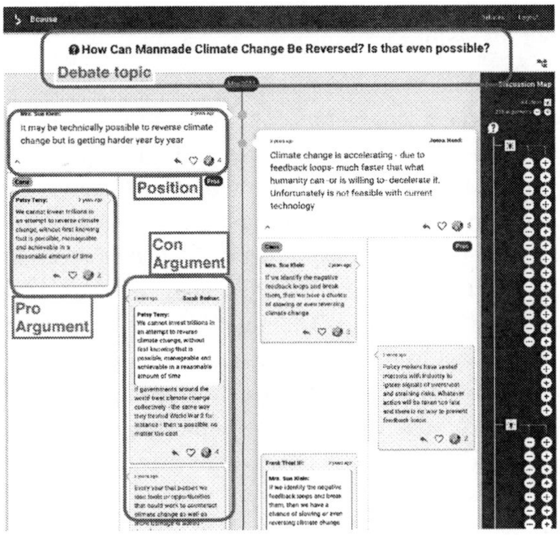

Figure 1: Argument-centric structure in BCause

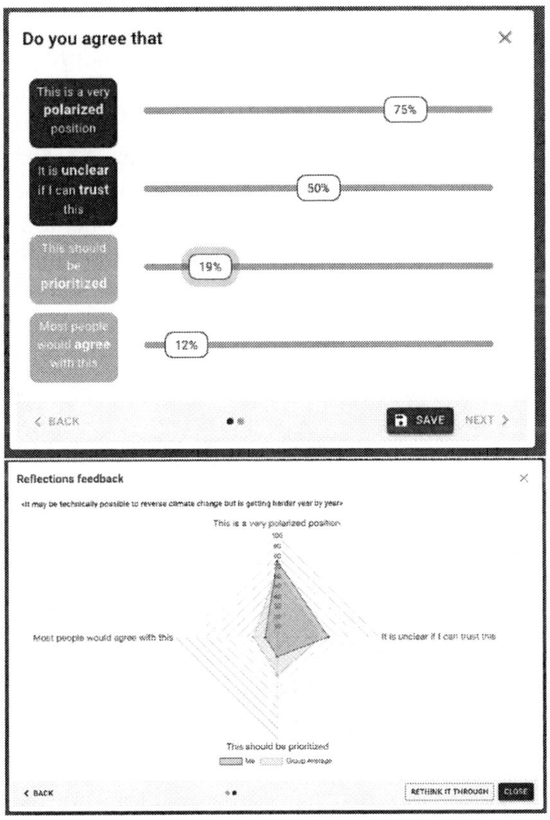

Figure 2: Reflection card two stage interaction

Figure 3: Reply dialog box and rendered "quoted" text within argument

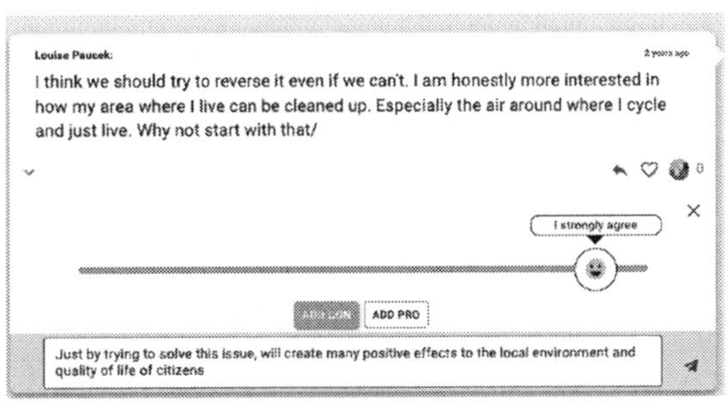

Figure 4: Argument input prologued by agreement slider

services, versus permitting people to make contributions with very little useful indexing or structure. Furthermore, since large scale discussions are hard to monitor and make sense of, our visual interfaces will be tailored to make sense and assess the state, progress and quality of a deliberation process. Towards this we aimed to explore new user interface paradigms to build usable but powerful technologies for highly usable deliberation on the Web.

To test our two main design solutions to the points **i**, **ii** above, we designed and focused our experiment to answer the following research questions:

RQ1: To what extent reflective feedback can improve engagement and sensemaking while reducing polarisation in argumentation-based discussions compared to appreciative feedback-only solutions?

RQ2: Can direct replies improve engagement but still avoiding polarisation, in argumentation-based discussions? And what is their effect on participants' engagement?

6 Methodology

To test those, we carried out an controlled A/B experiment with the four conditions:

- *Condition* **A**: this design variation contains a stripped down baseline - does not contain any of the agreement or reply buttons. It resembles a typical messaging platform (e.g. WhatsApp) where posts occur chronologically with no argumentation structure with also typical appreciative only feedback functionalities ("like" and "thank" you buttons).

- *Condition* **B**: In this design variation users' posts are organised in an argumentative fashion following an IBIS (Kunz and Rittel, 1970) approach, i.e. organising posts as positions and supporting or opposing arguments. The appreciative only feedback functionalities are retained.

- *Condition* **C**: Is an extension of condition B with more nuanced positive/negative feedback elements: i. agreement slider, ii. reflection feedback cards. From the appreciative only feedback elements we retain only the "like" button.

- *Condition* **D**: A full-fledged version containing all the elements of previous conditions (argumentative structuring, nuanced feedback) but also direct reply fucntionality.

6.1 Evaluation factors

We evaluated each condition against sensemaking and engagement factors. The chosen sensemaking features we used are an extract of Alsufiani et al. (2017) work on deducing theoretical features of Sensemaking, with an extra feature to assess Reflection (as defined by Weick (1995)) and proposed by De Liddo et al. (2021). Engagement factors are derived from O'Brien and Toms (2010) with adaptation to online discussion. Both are shown in Table 1 along with the question prompt given to crowdworkers. Note that some questions are given in negative form - this was later reversed in the analysis.

6.2 Experiment design

Each condition was tested in a group of 18 participants. To ensure limited bias we repeated the same trial three (3) times. In total, we recruited 216 participants (18 participants x 4 conditions x 3 trials). Users were recruited via Amazon Mechanical Turk and offered a compensation of 10$ per hour. We compared the discussion UI (3 different versions of it with argumentation structuring plus appreciative only feedbacks (condition B), structuring with nuanced positive/negative feedback (agreement slider plus reflection feedback cards (condition C), and full-fledged version (with structuring, nuanced feedback and reply (condition D)) against a "Whatsapp" like unthreaded discussion interface (condition A - used as a baseline). Participants were asked to contribute to a discussion that was pre-populated with 6 posts (in case of the argumentative conditions, 3 positions and 3 arguments). Within the group of 18, users could use other users' contributions as they were happening. For a task to be considered successful, at least 2 distinct contributions were expected (positions or arguments). Users were handed a post-hoc questionnaire with the questions presented in Table 1 in a 5-level Likert scale upon completion of the task.

7 Results

We present in Figure 5 the descriptive statistics of the 20 variables about engagement (11 factors) and sensemaking (9 factors) of the 3 design variations along with the control variation (group A). The box error plot data shows the average values of 3 separate trials of 18 participants each.

Code	Variable	Question
E1	Aesthetics	The platform is aesthetically appealing
E2	Perceived usability	I felt frustrated while trying to do some tasks
E3	Felt involvement	I felt involved in the discussion
E4	Perceived usability	I found the tool confusing to use
E5	Felt involvement	I was really drawn into the discussion
E6	Endurability	My experience discussing this topic did not evolve the way I would expect
E7	Focused attention	I was so involved in my task that I ignored everything around me
E8	Perceived usability	Using this website was mentally taxin
E9	Perceived usability	I felt in control of my discussion experience
E10	Perceived usability	I could not do some of the things I needed to do on the website
E11	Felt involvement	The discussion experience was fun
SM1	Reflection	I was able to reflect on the debated question
SM2	Insights	I was provided with unexpected insights on what is the question and what are the main arguments for and against
SM3	Focus	I was not able to focus on different aspects of the debate
SM4	Argumentation	I was able to find structure in the information provided in this debate and find a way to organise it
SM5	Explanation	I was not able to identify the main points raised in this debate
SM6	Assess Facts and evidence	I was able to assess facts and evidence provided in this debate
SM7	Distinguish	I was able to distinguish between different people's claims
SM8	Assess assumptions	I was not able to assess my initial assumptions about this debate
SM9	Change Assumptions	Some initial assumptions I had about this question changed

Table 1: Engagement and Sensemaking evaluation factors and corresponding question given to crowdworkers

To test variance homogeneity between the three separate 18-big batches, we ran a Levene's test (Gastwirth et al., 2009), which showed equal variance among the three samples. We proceeded then analysing all three batches in one unified 54-big sample. Upon affirming the normality of the data distribution through the application of the Shapiro-Wilk test ((Shapiro and Wilk, 1965)), we proceeded with ANOVA one-way analysis (Fisher, 1992), followed up by multiple pairwise comparisons employing Tukey's HSD ((Abdi and Williams, 2010)). The ANOVA analysis revealed no statistically significant differences among the factors, which was anticipated given the stringent Bonferroni correction ($a = 0.05/6$) applied to account for multiple comparisons. Nonetheless, it is noteworthy to mention that there was no degradation observed in the levels of Sensemaking and Engagement, a promising indication that the two interventions scrutinized (argument-structuring and reflective feedback elements) did not introduce cognitive load (information overload). The absence of an information overload due to the interventions as you could possibly expect, is reassuring for the seamless incorporation of those elements.

We then carried out a Social Network Analysis (SNA) on the interactions graph of each condition and evaluated network metrics, see results in Table 2. Social network analysis (SNA) can be employed in studies with a relatively small number of participants, like this one (n=18, 3 trials), particularly if interactions among the participants are expected to be complex and significantly interconnected. Even in such a small network, SNA can still provide valuable insights into the structure and properties of the network, such as the measurement of network fragmentation (Hanneman and Riddle, 2005). We observe that conditions C and D perform better in terms of average node degree and density. Average node degree is a good indication of Social Interaction coverage, basically how well the social interactions is distributed across the group. This indicates that the presence of argumentative discussion and cognitive reflection, produces a better social interaction. Network density is measure of the connectedness of the network in terms of total number of connections divided by the maximum possible number (of the perfectly interconnected graph) - so higher density means more interconnectedness.

Condition	A	B	C	D
# nodes	20.00	21.00	20.67	23.33
# edges	26.67	35.67	43.33	49.33
Average degree	2.68	3.40	4.18	4.29
Density	0.14	0.17	0.21	0.20
Diameter	4.00	5.67	5.00	5.50
Transitivity	0.16	0.17	0.23	0.26
Is connected?	1/3	3/3	3/3	2/3
Number of components	2.00	1.00	1.00	1.67
Largest component size	15.67	21.00	20.67	22.67
Largest component diameter	4.67	5.67	5.00	5.33

Table 2: Results of network analysis of conditions A,B,C and D. Metrics shown is the average over 3 trials.

Transitivity also slightly improves in conditions C and D. This means that the overall probability for the network to have adjacent nodes interconnected is higher, thus revealing the existence of more tightly connected communities. Transitivity number reflects the likelihood that the network's

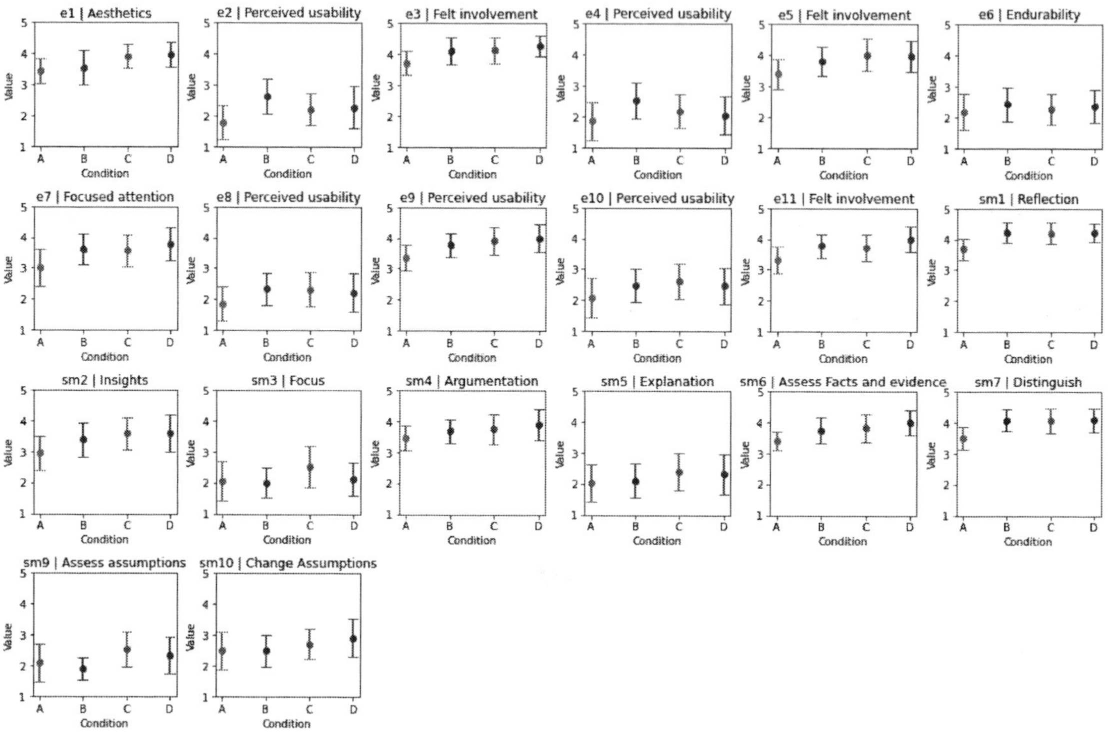

Figure 5: Results of 4 conditions across each engagement and Sensemaking factor

nodes form interconnected triads ((Opsahl, 2013)); which is interrelated to reciprocity (the tendency of pairs of nodes to be mutually linked). The comparatively large transitivity number posits an enhanced level of reciprocal engagement amongst users. Comparing the conditions with argumentative discussion (B,C,D) against condition A we also observe better connectiveness.

Number of components is the number of subgroups or tribes. Insertion of the argumentation structuring considerably reduce platform island (reduction of 2/3). The dimension of the largest component grows and reaches almost 89 percent of the total graph. Considering the largest component size metric combined with the largest component diameter, we can say that participants organised themselves around a large centric group rather than scatter to small isolated groups. This is a strong indication that argumentative discussion reduces the phenomenon of irregularities (islands of discussion) and promotes cohesive discussion.

8 Discussion

Though certain pathogens of democratic dialogue are not sourced in the implementation or design technotropy of social media or other discussion platforms but rather a certain reflection of the same problems in the virtual online environment, they are exacerbated within these platforms. Therefore complementary to technological solutions for democratic-aware design, ultimately the media and social literacy shall be pursued to address those problems. However in the interim and complementary, appropriate design solution for online discussion platforms should not be left unchecked and unaddressed.

For that we demonstrated that even seemingly small design decisions, have a significant impact on the dynamics of the discussion. Specifically, we showed that argumentation structuring is a viable and effective solution to many shortcomings of current social media technologies in supporting online deliberation. This is in line with previous research findings that structuring debates around issues and nudging participants have a positive effect, with no significant engagement drop (Tanasijevic and B"ohm, 2016).

Second, we showed that reflective appreciative feedback elements and reply interaction, equally abate some of the deficiencies of modern discussion platforms.

Overall our study findings inspire for a rebirth of

argument-centric solutions. After that we have observed an "argumentative winter" -if is permissible to employ this terminology- where people exibit distrust to argumentative technologies mainly because of the steep learning curve and low level engagement, we exhibit a solution that is comparable to typical social media, viable, feasible with equal if not better levels of engagement. This instils optimism of future solutions that will enable healthier and more civil deliberation.

Limitations

We recognise that our study has limitations. Firstly, the platform lacks elements that modern social media platform users take for granted, e.g. notifications, direct messaging, etc. Also, it was by design the absence of any moderation mechanism as we wanted to inspire a wide spectrum of opinions, even the extreme hyper-partisan views you would expect in an open platform (Oltmann et al., 2022). Further, the experiment executed to confirm our hypotheses was carried in a controlled environment with a predetermined interaction. We would expect that if reproduced in an open-ended environment several other phenomena stemming from network size, cold-start problems, user inertia or lack of trust would occur. However even though not a naturalistic setup, controlled experiment remains the best scientific device to establish a causal relationship between the examined variable and the user observed behaviour (Kohavi et al., 2007).

Acknowledgements

This research was funded by the U.S. Office of Naval Research under award number N00014-19-1-2366

References

A. Abbas, Y. Zhou, S. Deng, and P. Zhang. 2018. Text analytics to support sense-making in social media: A language-action perspective. *MIS Quarterly*, 42:2.

H. Abdi and L. J. Williams. 2010. Tukey's honestly significant difference (hsd) test. *Encyclopedia of research design*, 3(1):1–5.

K. Alsufiani, S. Attfield, and L. Zhang. 2017. Towards an instrument for measuring sensemaking and an assessment of its theoretical features.

Yair Amichai-Hamburger, Tali Gazit, Judit Bar-Ilan, Oren Perez, Noa Aharony, Jenny Bronstein, and Talia Sarah Dyne. 2016. Psychological factors behind the lack of participation in online discussions. *Computers in Human Behavior*, 55:268–277.

C. Bail. 2022. *Breaking the social media prism: How to make our platforms less polarizing*. Princeton University Press.

Richard Banfield, C Todd Lombardo, and Trace Wax. 2015. *Design sprint: A practical guidebook for building great digital products*. " O'Reilly Media, Inc.".

C. Barnett. 2003. *Culture and democracy: Media*. Edinburgh University Press, space and representation, Edinburgh, Scotland.

A. R. Binder, K. E. Dalrymple, D. Brossard, and D. A. Scheufele. 2009. The soul of a polarized democracy: Testing theoretical linkages between talk and attitude extremity during the 2004 presidential election. *Communication Research*, 36(3):315–340.

C. Blake and E. Scanlon. 2012. April. analysing collaborative processes and interaction patterns in online discussions. In *Eighth International Conference on Networked Learning 2012 (pp*, pages 2–04.

Kenneth Boyd. 2023. Group epistemology and structural factors in online group polarization. *Episteme*, 20(1):57–72.

Lucas Carstens, Xiuyi Fan, Yang Gao, and Francesca Toni. 2015. An overview of argumentation frameworks for decision support. In *Graph Structures for Knowledge Representation and Reasoning: 4th International Workshop, GKR 2015, Buenos Aires, Argentina, July 25, 2015, Revised Selected Papers 4*, pages 32–49. Springer.

S. Coleman and G. Moss. 2012. Under construction: The field of online deliberation research. *Journal of information technology & politics*, 9(1):1–15.

G. Collison, B. Elbaum, S. Haavind, and R. Tinker. 2000. Facilitating online learning: Effective strategies for moderators. *Atwood Publishing, Madison, WI, USA*, 1:89185.

J. Conklin. 2008. Growing a global issue base: An issue-based approach to policy deliberation. In *n proceeding of: Directions and Implications of Advanced Computing; Conference on Online Deliberation*, 2008. University of California, Berkeley.

A. De Liddo, N. P. Souto, and B. Pl"uss. 2021. Let's replay the political debate: Hypervideo technology for visual sensemaking of televised election debates. *International Journal of Human-Computer Studies*, 145.

M. Dean. 1999. *Governmentality: Power and rule in modern society*. SAGE, Thousand Oaks, CA.

P. H. Ditto and D. F. Lopez. 1992. Motivated skepticism: Use of differential decision criteria for preferred and nonpreferred conclusions. *Journal of personality and social psychology*, 63:4.

Aviad Elyashar, Jorge Bendahan, and Rami Puzis. 2017a. Is the online discussion manipulated? quantifying the online discussion authenticity within online social media. *arXiv preprint arXiv:1708.02763*.

Aviad Elyashar, Jorge Bendahan, Rami Puzis, and Maria-Amparo Sanmateu. 2017b. Measurement of online discussion authenticity within online social media. In *Proceedings of the 2017 IEEE/ACM International Conference on Advances in Social Networks Analysis and Mining 2017*, pages 627–629.

Ronald Aylmer Fisher. 1992. *Statistical methods for research workers*. Springer.

A. France. 2017. Cass r. *Sunstein:# Republic: Divided Democracy in the Age of Social Media*, 20(5):1091–1093.

Batya Friedman, Peter Kahn, and Alan Borning. 2002. Value sensitive design: Theory and methods. *University of Washington technical report*, 2:12.

D. Friess and C. Eilders. 2015. A systematic review of online deliberation research. *Policy & Internet*, 7(3):319–339.

J. L. Gastwirth, Y. R. Gel, and W. Miao. 2009. The impact of Levene's test of equality of variances on statistical theory and practice.

Patricia K Gilbert and Nada Dabbagh. 2005. How to structure online discussions for meaningful discourse: A case study. *British Journal of Educational Technology*, 36(1):5–18.

Jennifer Golbeck, Zahra Ashktorab, Rashad O Banjo, Alexandra Berlinger, Siddharth Bhagwan, Cody Buntain, Paul Cheakalos, Alicia A Geller, Quint Gergory, Rajesh Kumar Gnanasekaran, et al. 2017. A large labeled corpus for online harassment research. In *Proceedings of the 2017 ACM on web science conference*, pages 229–233.

S. C. Guntuku, D. B. Yaden, M. L. Kern, L. H. Ungar, and J. C. Eichstaedt. 2017. Detecting depression and mental illness on social media: an integrative review. *Current Opinion in Behavioral Sciences*, 18:43–49.

Robert A Hanneman and Mark Riddle. 2005. Introduction to social network methods.

Noriko Hara, Curtis Jay Bonk, and Charoula Angeli. 2000. Content analysis of online discussion in an applied educational psychology course. *Instructional science*, 28:115–152.

R. R. Huckfeldt and J. Sprague. 1995. *Citizens, politics and social communication: Information and influence in an election campaign*. Cambridge University Press.

L. Iandoli, S. Primario, and G. Zollo. 2021. The impact of group polarization on the quality of online debate in social media: A systematic literature review. *Technological Forecasting and Social Change*, 170.

M. Klein and L. Iandoli. 2008. Supporting collaborative deliberation using a large-scale. In *Argumentation System: The MIT Collaboratorium*. University of California, Berkeley, Directions and Implications of Advanced. Computing; Conference on Online Deliberation. 2008.

R. Kohavi, R. M. Henne, and D. Sommerfield. 2007. Practical guide to controlled experiments on the web: listen to your customers not to the hippo. In *Proceedings of the 13th ACM SIGKDD international conference on Knowledge discovery and data mining*, pages 959–967.

W. Kunz and H. W. Rittel. 1970. *Issues as elements of information systems (Vol. 131, p. 14)*. Institute of Urban and Regional Development, University of California, Berkeley, CA.

J. Law and J. Urry. 2004. Enacting the social. *Economy and Society*, 33(3):40–53.

S. Lewandowsky, L. Smillie, D. Garcia, R. Hertwig, J. Weatherall, S. Egidy, R. E. Robertson, C. O'Connor, A. Kozyreva, P. Lorenz-Spreen, and Y. Blaschke. 2020. Understanding the influence of online technologies on political behaviour and decision-making, Technology and democracy.

J Nathan Matias, Amy Johnson, Whitney Erin Boesel, Brian Keegan, Jaclyn Friedman, and Charlie DeTar. 2015. Reporting, reviewing, and responding to harassment on twitter. *arXiv preprint arXiv:1505.03359*.

Paula San Millan Maurino. 2007. Looking for critical thinking in online threaded discussions. *Journal of Educational Technology Systems*, 35(3):241–260.

D. C. Mutz. 2001. Facilitating communication across lines of political difference: The role of mass media. *American political science review*, 95(1):97–114.

D. C. Mutz. 2002. Cross-cutting social networks: Testing democratic theory in practice. *American Political Science Review*, 96(1):111–126.

Manuela Neurauter-Kessels. 2013. *Impoliteness in cyberspace: Personally abusive reader responses in online news media*. Ph.D. thesis, University of Zurich.

H. L. O'Brien and E. G. Toms. 2010. The development and evaluation of a survey to measure user engagement. *Journal of the American Society for Information Science and Technology*, 61(1):50–69.

K. O'Leary, J. O. Wobbrock, and E. A. Riskin. 2013. April. In *Q-Methodology as a Research and Design Tool for HCI*, pages 1941–1950. of the SIGCHI Conference on Human Factors in Computing Systems.

S. M. Oltmann, E. J. Knox, and M. N. Mabi. 2022. Censorship is not a panacea: Access to information in a resilient society. In *Proceedings of the Association for Information Science and Technology*, pages 591–594. 59.

Tore Opsahl. 2013. Triadic closure in two-mode networks: Redefining the global and local clustering coefficients. *Social networks*, 35(2):159–167.

S. S. Shapiro and M. B. Wilk. 1965. An analysis of variance test for normality (complete samples). *Biometrika*, 52(3):591–611.

Aaron Shaw and Eszter Hargittai. 2018. The pipeline of online participation inequalities: The case of wikipedia editing. *Journal of communication*, 68(1):143–168.

Ruth Shortall, Anatol Itten, Michiel van der Meer, Pradeep K Murukannaiah, and Catholijn M Jonker. 2021. Inclusion, equality and bias in designing online mass deliberative platforms. *arXiv preprint arXiv:2107.12711*.

Kim Strandberg, Staffan Himmelroos, and Kimmo Grönlund. 2019. Do discussions in like-minded groups necessarily lead to more extreme opinions? deliberative democracy and group polarization. *International Political Science Review*, 40(1):41–57.

Cass Sunstein. 2018. # republic. In *# Republic*. Princeton university press.

C. S. Taber and M. Lodge. 2006. Motivated skepticism in the evaluation of political beliefs. *American journal of political science*, 50(3):755–769.

S. Tanasijevic and K. B"ohm. 2016. Towards effective structure-based assessment of proposals and arguments in online deliberation. *International Journal of Systems and Service-Oriented Engineering (IJSSOE)*, 6(2):29–52.

D. Walton. 2005. *Fundamentals of critical argumentation*. Cambridge University Press.

Y. M. Wang. 2019. Enhancing the quality of online discussion—assessment matters. *Journal of Educational Technology Systems*, 48(1):112–129.

K. E. Weick. 1995. *Sensemaking in organizations (Vol. 3)*. Sage.

A. X. (2017 Zhang. October). systems for improving online discussion. In *Adjunct Publication of the 30th Annual ACM Symposium on User Interface Software and Technology*, pages 111–114.

Measuring Lexico-Semantic Alignment in Debates with Contextualized Word Representations

Aina Garí Soler, Matthieu Labeau, Chloé Clavel
LTCI, Télécom-Paris, Institut Polytechnique de Paris, France
{aina.garisoler,matthieu.labeau,chloe.clavel}@telecom-paris.fr

Abstract

Dialog participants sometimes align their linguistic styles, e.g., they use the same words and syntactic constructions as their interlocutors. We propose to investigate the notion of lexico-semantic alignment: to what extent do speakers convey the same meaning when they use the same words? We design measures of lexico-semantic alignment relying on contextualized word representations. We show that they reflect interesting semantic differences between the two sides of a debate and that they can assist in the task of debate's winner prediction.

1 Introduction

It is well known that dialog participants often tend to imitate each other. This phenomenon, known as alignment or entrainment, can be of a linguistic nature (lexical (Brennan and Clark, 1996), syntactic (Branigan et al., 2000), prosodic (Street Jr, 1984)...) and it has also been observed in non-linguistic behavior such as posture (Shockley et al., 2003) or visual attention (Richardson et al., 2008). For example, throughout a conversation, speakers may reuse the lexical items used by their partners (Nenkova et al., 2008), and they tend to use the same referring expressions to refer to the same entities (Brennan and Clark, 1996). This mechanism is said to facilitate language production and comprehension in the interaction (Pickering and Garrod, 2004); and lexical and syntactic repetition have been found to correlate with task success in task-oriented dialog (Reitter and Moore, 2007).

One kind of alignment that is less often addressed in the literature is conceptual alignment (Stolk et al., 2016). This refers to the extent to which two dialog participants "mean the same things when using the same words" (Schober, 2005). The fact that words have pre-established senses does not guarantee conceptual alignment, as speakers may have slightly different mental representations of words (e.g., different associations,

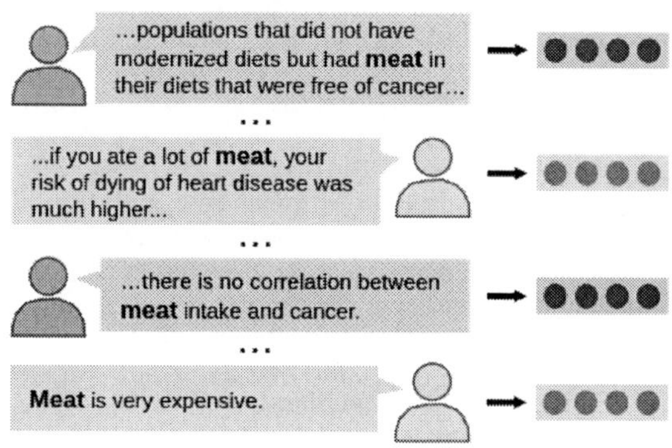

Figure 1: We identify words that are used by both sides in a debate (here, *meat*) and extract contextualized representations from all their instances, which are then compared through our alignment measures. Example from the IQ2 dataset (Zhang et al., 2016).

connotations, or a different level of detail), use them differently, or propose novel usages.

While it has been found that alignment at one level enhances alignment at other levels (Cleland and Pickering, 2003; Pickering and Garrod, 2004), lexical (or surface form) alignment may actually mask conceptual misalignment, which, if undetected, can lead to serious misunderstandings (Schober, 2005).[1] Nevertheless, conceptual (mis)alignment remains understudied, mainly because it is hard to detect.

In this paper, we target a more restricted notion of conceptual alignment: we seek to quantify the divergence or convergence of word meaning that is inferrable from textual information alone, i.e., from the way the same words are used by two speakers throughout a dialog (see Figure 1). We do not intend to capture conceptual misalignments that are made apparent only through non-linguistic

[1] People responding to the same survey twice in the space of a week were twice more likely to change their answers (22% vs 11%) if interviewers had the right to provide clarifications the second time around (Conrad and Schober, 2000). The change in responses indicates that the additional explanations helped uncover and correct an initial conceptual misalignment.

Proceedings of the First Workshop on Social Influence in Conversations (SICon 2023), pages 50–63
July 14, 2023 ©2023 Association for Computational Linguistics

behavior or which involve external referents (e.g., someone performing the wrong action after misunderstanding a command). We refer to this notion as **lexico-semantic alignment**.

We propose, for the first time, a methodology and a set of metrics to explore and quantify lexico-semantic alignment in its definition presented above. Our metrics rely on contextualized word representations, which have been found to reflect different aspects of word meaning, including connotation (Garí Soler et al., 2022). We work with a corpus of two-sided debates which constitutes a scenario with interesting dynamics where we can find opinion disparity as well as concessions from either side. The application of an automatic coreference solver additionally allows us to work with different surface forms referring to the same entity. We carry out a qualitative and quantitative analysis of the proposed measures and investigate their usefulness in predicting a debate's outcome. Our measures reflect interesting word usage discrepancies between debate sides, and are directly applicable to other kinds of conversations.[2]

2 Related Work

2.1 Conceptual and Semantic Alignment

The first evidence of the tendency of speakers to align conceptually comes from Garrod and Anderson (1987) who noted that "once speakers have established a particular interpretation for an expression ... they try to avoid any potentially ambiguous use of that expression". Markman and Makin (1998) found that communication served to synchronize categorization (and thus to increase conceptual alignment): people who had worked together in a task involving toy construction pieces would sort pieces more similarly than two people who had collaborated on the task without talking.

Very few studies attempt to quantify conceptual alignment between dialog participants using automatic tools. Babcock et al. (2014); Ta et al. (2017) and Vrana et al. (2018) calculate the Latent Semantic Similarity (LSS, Landauer and Dumais 1997) between two speakers in a conversation. They find that LSS correlates positively with multiple dialog-level variables related to conversation length, expressive gestures or positive affect, among others. Xu (2021) uses more modern utterance representations derived from contextualized and static word representations (e.g., BERT (Devlin et al., 2019) and GloVe (Pennington et al., 2014)) to track utterance similarity throughout a dialog. The author finds patterns of global divergence and local convergence: semantic distance increases with temporal distance. These studies, however, compare the semantics of full utterances. We, instead, use contextualized word representations derived from BERT to compare how each side of a conversation uses a specific word. We partially follow work by Garí Soler et al. (2022), which compares word instance representations from sentences expressing opposing standpoints, and extend it to the two sides of a debate.

2.2 Asymmetric Alignment

We have so far described alignment as a mutual effort towards convergence, but one speaker can show more willingness to align than the other due to, among others, an asymmetry in their interpersonal relationship. For example, Danescu-Niculescu-Mizil et al. (2012) find that "higher-power" speakers (e.g., Wikipedia editors with Administrator status) receive more alignment (in terms of linguistic style markers used) than those of lower power. Xu et al. (2018), however, claim that this observation can be explained by low-level linguistic features such as utterance length, which tends to be larger in higher-power speakers and promotes a stronger alignment.

Asymmetric alignment has been observed in the context of debates, too. An electoral candidate's higher ranking in polls has been found to correlate with their convergence to the opponent's style (Romero et al., 2015) and the frequence with which the candidate manages to introduce or shift a topic (Prabhakaran et al., 2014). Similarly, Zhang et al. (2016) identify talking points of each side of a debate and investigate the extent to which each side talks about its own points or the opponent's points. They find that the winners tend to exhibit a drop in self-coverage, and are also more active in addressing the opponent's points.

In this study, we present both symmetric and asymmetric alignment measures. Relying on the same dataset as Zhang et al. (2016), we test the usefulness of asymmetric measures in predicting the winner of a debate.

[2]Our code is available at `https://github.com/ainagari/LSalignment`.

3 Data and Preprocessing

In this section we explain how we find the common vocabulary between debate sides and how we extract contextualized representations for words and phrases in this shared vocabulary.

3.1 Dataset

We use the Intelligence Squared Debates corpus (Zhang et al., 2016), IQ2, which contains 108 debates.[3] In each debate D there are two teams or sides ($S = \{f, a\}$), *f*or and *a*gainst the motion being discussed, made up of 2-3 people. Every debate has three parts: an introduction where each panelist is invited to present their main points in eight minutes; a 30-minute interactive part with questions from the moderator and the audience, and a conclusion where every participant has two minutes to make a closing statement. The audience casts a vote (for, against or undecided) before the debate and during the conclusion part. A team is considered to win a debate if it managed to "convert" more people, i.e., if the difference in the percentage of votes that their side received after vs before the debate is larger than that of the other team.

3.2 Shared Words

We are interested in observing the usage of words that are common to the two sides of a debate. We pos-tag and lemmatize[4] all the data. Following Garí Soler et al. (2022), we consider only nouns and verbs that are used at least three times by each side and for which all measures can be calculated.[5] We exclude stopwords and punctuation. We refer to the full shared vocabulary in a debate D as $V(D)$.

We additionally calculate tf-idf scores for every lemma, treating every debate as a document and determining the idf term from the whole dataset. We use these scores to select the most relevant and topic-specific words in a debate to be included in our analysis. See Table 5 (Appendix B) for examples of words ranked by tf-idf. Unless otherwise specified, we only use lemmas in $V(D)$ that are included in the top 200 by tf-idf ($V_{t200}(D)$). More information on the final vocabulary size used is given in Section 5.

[3]Available with the convokit library (Chang et al., 2020).

[4]We use the nltk library.

[5]As explained in Section 4.2, certain measures have additional restrictions on the required number of instances.

3.3 Shared Entities

Coreference is a strongly present phenomenon in dialog, where speakers continously refer to already introduced entities with the use of pronouns, anaphoric expressions or paraphrases. Including chains of coreferent mentions in our analysis allows us to have a more complete and realistic picture of everything that is said about an entity, regardless of the way speakers refer to it. It also allows us to investigate the specific lexical choices made by each side, which may carry different connotations.[6]

We use the model presented by the UTD_NLP team (Li et al., 2022) at the recent CODI-CRAC 2022 shared task (Yu et al., 2022) which concerned anaphora phenomena in dialog. This was the best-performing coreference solver, with a 75.04 average CONLL F1 score on task 1 (identity anaphora resolution). We feed the model the full debates, including utterances by the moderator, the host and the audience. As a result we obtain coreference chains of terms referring to the same entity or concept.

We only include in our analysis those coreference chains with at least 3 co-referring terms uttered by each team. We observe that chains containing references to the panelists tend to contain errors, particularly when it comes to pronouns. This is understandable, as in a multi-party conversation it is not always clear who a speaker is referring to, especially from text alone. While it would be interesting to analyze how panelists talk about and refer to each other, we omit these chains from our analysis in order to reduce the errors due to automatic prediction.[7] After this filtering, we find an average of 16.3 coreference chains per debate, with an average length of 30.2[8] instances, which complete $V(D)$. We refer to this subset of the vocabulary as $V_C(D)$, and to the complementary subset made of lemmas as $V_W(D)$. Table 6 (Appendix B) shows examples of the coreference solver's output, which captures the use of synonyms, pronouns, phrases and paraphrases.

[6]E.g., "Mexico's drug war" vs "America's drug war" as a way of emphasizing a party's responsibility or the war's reach or scope (example from the debate on "America Is To Blame For Mexico's Drug War").

[7]We automatically omit chains where one instance coincides with a panelist's full name, as well as all chains that are predominantly ($\geq 70\%$) made up of 1st and 2nd person pronouns.

[8]Counts do not include instances uttered by the host or the moderator.

3.4 Representation Extraction

Following Garí Soler et al. (2022), we extract contextualized representations for words and entities from BERT's (base, uncased) 10th layer. When a word is split into multiple tokens, we average the representations of each token. Since mentions in coreference chains can have multiple surface forms and BERT is sensitive to orthographic differences (Laicher et al., 2021), we additionally try using masking. We test different masking strategies to see which one yields representations that better reflect the differences in opinion between opposing sides. This experiment is detailed in Appendix A; as not masking gave the best result, all analyses presented in what follows are carried out without masking. We denote the set of instances of a word[9] $w \in V(D)$ uttered by a specific side $s \in S$ as $I_{w,s}$. We refer to the contextualized representation of an instance $i \in I_{w,s}$ as $\overrightarrow{i}$.

4 Alignment Measures

We propose measures which reflect different aspects of lexico-semantic alignment and compare them to lexical alignment measures used in previous work. We use a debate entitled "Don't Eat Anything With A Face"[10] as a running example to show the ranking of words obtained with each measure in Table 1. This table is to be discussed in more detail in Section 5.1. We compare the two sides of a debate, but our measures can be used to compare the word usages of two individual speakers.

We distinguish two main types of measures. With time-unaware (TU) measures, we compare word representations obtained from the debate as a whole, without taking into account the evolution or the change in word meaning as the debate progresses. Time-aware (TA) metrics, instead, explicitly compare representations at different temporal points of the debate. We make an additional distinction between symmetric and asymmetric measures. The former are measures of global or general alignment, whereas the latter are calculated separately for each side. We also consider measures of self-alignment, which quantify the semantic variation within a side.

[9] Here, a "word" is understood as a lemma with a specific PoS or as a concept described by a coreference chain. An "instance" is a specific usage of a word in context.

[10] This debate is clearly won by side FOR, which collects 21 additional votes after the debate, as opposed to AGAINST, which loses 8 votes.

Several of our measures rely on the averaged pairwise similarities ($psim$) between the representations of two sets of instances I and J (Equation 1). sim corresponds to a similarity measure. Unless otherwise specified, we use cosine similarity. It can be replaced with a distance measure, such as the Euclidean distance, in which case the results need to be interpreted accordingly.

$$psim(I, J) = \frac{\sum_{i \in I} \sum_{j \in J} sim(\overrightarrow{i}, \overrightarrow{j})}{|I| \times |J|} \quad (1)$$

4.1 Time-Unaware (TU) Measures

TU Self-Similarity (SS_{TU}) This metric measures the amount of variation that there is in the way one side of a debate uses one word. The SS_{TU} of a word w used by side s is calculated as the average pairwise similarity of instances within $I_{w,s}$:

$$SS_{TU}(w, s) = \frac{\sum_{i \in I_{w,s}} \sum_{i' \in I_{w,s}, i' \neq i} sim(\overrightarrow{i}, \overrightarrow{i'})}{|I_{w,s}|^2 - |I_{w,s}|} \quad (2)$$

With this metric we can examine the words that show the most and the least variation across sides (see Table 1). A global $SS_{TU}(s)$ measure for a side s of a debate D can be calculated by averaging the $SS_{TU}(s, w)$ of all words $w \in V(D)$.

TU Other-Similarity (OS_{TU}) This measure quantifies the similarity between the representation of a word w by each side in the debate. It gives an idea of how similar the meaning or the usage of a word is between the two sides.

$$OS_{TU}(w) = psim(I_{w,f}, I_{w,a}) \quad (3)$$

$OS_{TU}(w)$ allows us to see what words were the most and the least differently used between sides in the debate as a whole. We can calculate $OS_{TU}(D)$ for the whole debate by averaging the $OS_{TU}(w)$ of all words $w \in V(D)$.

Shared Vocabulary (SV) for a given concept We want to quantify the degree to which the two sides use the same surface forms to talk about the same thing. A given coreference chain $w \in V_C(D)$ consists of a set of instances uttered by either side (I_w). An instance $i \in I_w$ is realized with a specific surface form or realization r_i. The set of different realizations observed for chain w is denoted as R_w. To calculate this measure for a specific coreference chain ($SV(w)$), we first omit all mentions in I_w

that consist of a single pronoun. We only proceed if after this operation $|I_{w,s}| > 3$ for each side s.

We observe that chains often contain mentions that are very similar in form (e.g., *the war on drugs* vs *the drug war*). To avoid counting these as different realizations of the same concept, we perform a preliminary clustering of mentions in R_w based on their pairwise Levenshtein distance. Specifically, we merge realizations that are similar in form by means of hierarchical clustering with average linkage using a threshold of 5. After this step, expressions such as *this war* and *the war* are considered to be equivalent ways of referring to the concept expressed by w. Finally, we calculate the overlap between the two sides as follows:

$$SV(w) = \frac{\sum_{r \in R_w} min(|\{i \in I_{w,s} : r_i = r\}|, |\{j \in I_{w,s'} : r_j = r\}|)}{min(|I_{w,s}|, |I_{w,s'}|)} \quad (4)$$

$SV(w)$ ranges from 0 (no overlap) to 1 (maximum overlap). To be able to fairly compare the overlap of different coreference chains in the same debate, the score is normalized by the total number of instances involving concepts in $V_C(D)$:

$$SV(w, D) = SV(w) \frac{|I_w|}{\sum_{w' \in V_C(D)} |I_{w'}|} \quad (5)$$

This is the only measure that does not rely on contextualized representations. Despite the focus on surface form, we still consider it as a lexico-semantic measure because it is meant to be computed only on semantically equivalent expressions.

4.2 Time-Aware (TA) Measures

The metrics proposed here assume the existence of (at least) two time steps, an initial t_k and a posterior t_{k+1}. The set of instances of a word w by side s at time step k is denoted as $I_{w,s,k}$. We divide every debate into two halves (or time steps) following the number of tokens.[11] To calculate these measures for w, we require at least one instance of w per side and time step.

TA Self-Similarity (SS_{TA}) Analogously to SS_{TU}, this measure describes the self-variation of a word's usage within one side of the debate. SS_{TA}, however, takes time into account: we compare the representations at the beginning (t_k) and the end (t_{k+1}) of the debate to see if word usage has changed. While SS_{TU} represents the overall variation within one side, SS_{TA} captures evolution.

$$SS_{TA}(w, s) = psim(I_{w,s,k}, I_{w,s,k+1}) \quad (6)$$

Symmetric Approaching ($sApp$) This measure indicates whether the two sides came to use the word in a more similar way towards the end of the debate as opposed to the beginning. It is the difference in similarity between the two sides across the two time steps:

$$sApp(w) = psim(I_{w,f,k+1}, I_{w,a,k+1}) - psim(I_{w,f,k}, I_{w,a,k}) \quad (7)$$

A positive value means that representations of the two sides became closer by the end of the debate, compared to how they were at the beginning. Negative values indicate they grew further apart. The absolute value quantifies the magnitude of this difference.

Asymmetric Approaching ($asApp$) The measures introduced so far only tell us how close or similar representations are, or how much they approached each other. If the representations from the two sides are farther apart from each other at the end of the debate, what is the team that took the initiative of, or contributed the most to, this distancing? As explained in Section 2.2, Zhang et al. (2016) found that the winners of a debate tend to address the topics raised by their opponents. In a similar vein, we hypothesize that a side's initiative in approaching the other could be related to its outcome in the debate. To obtain a measure that reflects how much a side s has approached the other (s') in their usage of a word w, we take into consideration whether the representations by side s at t_{k+1} have come closer to the w representations from the other side s' at the previous time step:

$$sApp(w, s) = psim(I_{w,s,k+1}, I_{w,s',k}) - psim(I_{w,s,k}, I_{w,s',k}) \quad (8)$$

$asApp(w, s)$ is positive if the most recent word instances by side s ($I_{w,s,k+1}$) are closer in meaning to the initial instances of the word by the opposite side ($I_{w,s',k}$) than s's initial usage of w ($I_{w,s,k}$), and it is negative if they are farther away. We assume that the representations at time t_0 express the initial, unbiased meaning of a word by each side, whereas

[11] We considered the use of a sliding window, but discarded it due to data scarcity – most words do not occur in most windows. We leave the search for more sophisticated ways of taking temporality into account for future work.

			FOR	AGAINST
Time-Unaware	SS_{TU}	most similar	anything, farming, vegan, factory, attack	face, meat, farming, human, cancer
		least similar	life, grow, cow, die, study	attack, life, anything, die, study
	OS_{TU}	most similar	face, factory, meat, farming, cancer, human, vegetarian, vegan, animal, vegetable	
		least similar	life, attack, grow, die, study, cow, health, kill, fat, heart	
	SV	most overlap	fish, corn, plants, the globe / the world / the planet, vegetarians, face, cancer	
		least overlap	vitamin B12 / B12, the nation / the country, humans / human beings, this motion / the resolution	
Time-Aware	SS_{TA}	least evolved	anything, farming, vegan, factory, soil	face, cancer, cow, meat, human
		most evolved	grow, cow, life, die, kill	life, attack, study, health, die
	$sApp$	most approached	cow, grow, attack, anything, face, life, die, corn, meat, eat	
		most distanced	study, fat, vegetarian, health, soil, plant, food, farming, farm	
	$asApp$	most approached	cow, grow, face, human, attack	anything, attack, vegetable, eat, meat
		most distanced	vegetarian, fat, study, vegan, farming	study, health, food, plant, soil
	DS	common approaching	(+ balanced) factory, corn, attack, meat ... life, vegetable, cow, animal (- balanced)	
		common distancing	health, study, plant	
		opposite behavior	(+ extreme) diet$_f$, farm$_a$, food$_f$, farming$_a$ ... vegan$_a$, kill$_f$, grow$_f$, eat$_a$ (- extreme)	

Table 1: Word rankings obtained on the debate "Don't Eat Anything With A Face" by each measure: Time-unaware Self- and Other-Similarity (SS_{TU}, OS_{TU}), Shared Vocabulary (SV), Time-aware Self-Similarity (SS_{TA}), Symmetric and Asymmetric Approaching ($sApp$, $asApp$) and Driving Strength (DS). We use $V_{t200}(D)$ (28 words) (or $V_C(D)$ with 12 chains for SV). In DS (opposite behavior), subscripts indicate the side that approached.

representations at a posterior time step t_{k+1} reflect the evolution of the meaning of this word after having heard the other side. This measure indicates whether, and how much, the meaning of a word got closer to the pure, initial meaning of the word as presented by the other side. In this sense, it can capture the influence that the other side's statements may have had on s's representation of a word.

Driving Strength (DS) We combine the $asApp$ obtained by each side to obtain a normalized measure that indicates how much of the total approaching (or distancing) done by both sides each team is responsible for:

$$DS(w, s) = \frac{asApp(w, s)}{|asApp(w, s)| + |asApp(w, s')|} \quad (9)$$

$DS(w, s)$ can range between -1 and 1. Similarly to $asApp$, it is positive if s at t_{k+1} approached s' at t_k, and negative otherwise. For example, if $DS(w, s) = 0.5$ and $DS(w, s') = -0.5$, it means that both sides travelled the same distance, but s approached s' and s' got farther away from s. In this case, $sApp(w)$ would be 0, which would not reflect the fact that one side approached the other.

To sum up, we have three symmetric measures, two time-unaware (OS_{TU}, SV) and one time-aware ($sApp$); and four asymmetric measures, one time-unaware (SS_{TU}) and three time-aware (SS_{TA}, $asApp$ and DS). See Figure 2 in Appendix B for an illustration of how each measure behaves in different situations.

4.3 Lexical Measures

We calculate a series of measures available from the Dialign software (Dubuisson Duplessis et al., 2021) which take into account different aspects of lexical alignment (amount of self-/other-repetition, variety of expressions, complexity of lexical patterns, orientation of alignment...). We provide a list of the metrics in Appendix C. A more thorough description can be found in Dubuisson Duplessis et al. (2021). We include these measures to investigate the correlation between lexical and lexico-semantic alignment, and to combine them with our proposed measures for predicting a debate's winning side.

5 Analysis

In Section 5.1, we carry out a qualitative analysis of the kinds of phenomena our measures reflect. We do so following our running example and looking at the results for individual words presented in Table 1. Section 5.2 investigates the measures' behavior when calculated at the dataset level.

The vocabulary used for the SV metric is $V_C(D)$. For all other metrics, we use word lemmas from $V_{t200}(D)$ provided that at least one instance is available for each time step and side.[12] This consists of 33 lemmas on average.

[12] This restriction is not necessary for time-unaware metrics, but we apply it so the same vocabulary is used across all measures.

5.1 Word-level Analysis

We find that our measures, calculated with BERT, capture a wide range of usage phenomena. Apart from differences in word sense (WS) and connotation (CN), they are also sensitive to unusual word usages or expressions (U), to differences in collocations or subject/object preferences (CL), and to the distinction between entities and common nouns (E). We present several examples below.

In Table 1, we can see that the noun *attack* has one of the lowest OS_{TU}. This reflects the fact that FOR talks exclusively about heart attacks related to meat consumption, whereas AGAINST also mentions panic attacks (due to a worse mental health presumably caused by veganism) and attacks in a metaphorical sense ("Being vegan is an attack on the poor") **(WS)**. This also explains why SS_{TU}(*attack*, *f*) is quite high. Another word with low OS_{TU} is *die*: while AGAINST talks more often about animals dying, FOR also mentions people dying from diseases related to elevated meat consumption **(CL)**. *Factory*, instead, has a high OS_{TU}, and it is used by both sides almost exclusively in the context of "factory farm" **(CL)**.

Farming displays a very high SS_{TU} for FOR. This is because its instances almost exclusively contain criticism to factory farming (e.g., "factory farming is an abomination", "factory farming is bad") **(CN, CL)**. *Life*, instead, is one of the words with highest variation within both sides of the debate. Both FOR and AGAINST indeed make a varied use of this word: to talk about animals' or humans' life, to talk about killing ("taking someone's life"), about health ("life expectancy"), or to refer to "aliveness" in general ("life often comes from death") **(WS, CL)**.

When it comes to *sApp*, we find that *vegetarian* is among the words that became most distant between sides. This is because in the debate, AGAINST starts talking about their failed past as a vegetarian and the benefits that they expected from it. But beyond that, instances of *vegetarian* by each side occur in sentences that highlight the benefits of the dietary choice (meat-based vs vegetarian) that is being defended or the problems created by the opposing side's choice **(CN)**. In the case of *study*, also with low $sApp$, FOR focuses on a specific study called "the China study" during the second half, whereas in the rest of the debate both sides bring up multiple studies in a similar way **(E, CL)**.

Cow and *grow*, instead, are two of the words whose representation becomes most similar. FOR uses *cow* in the expression "Holy cow" in the first part of the debate, but its subsequent usages are literal (i.e., not idiomatic), like those by AGAINST **(U)**. *Grow* is used with the meaning of "growing up" by FOR in the first half, while in the rest of the debate it tends to be used in the sense of growing crops **(WS)**. *Anything* and *face*, both with high $sApp$, are two words included in the title of the motion, which is repeated multiple times throughout the debate **(CL)**. However, *face* is initially used by FOR to talk about empathy when looking into someone else's face, which explains the high value of $asApp(face, f)$. The case of *corn* is also interesting: its high $sApp$ can be attributed to an unusual usage of *corn* by AGAINST in the first half ("corn has ears"), to refer to the fact that plants are sentient. FOR picks up on this on the second half of the debate ("not one ear of that corn is going to be eaten") **(U)**.

Looking at the coreference chains and their shared vocabulary SV between sides, we do not observe anything particularly controversial in this debate. When talking about humans, AGAINST uses mostly *humans*, pronouns (*we* and *our*, which are not taken into account in our measure) or, in one occasion, *human beings*. FOR uses also *mankind*, *man* and *people*. FOR very often refers to vitamin B12 simply as *B12*, whereas AGAINST uses the whole phrase.

We also calculate the correlation between our measures and word frequency, counted as the number of occurrences of a word in a debate as a whole (for symmetric measures) and by side (for asymmetric ones). Results show that none of our measures is affected by frequency ($|\rho| < 0.04$).

5.2 Dataset-level Analysis

In Table 2, we present the descriptive statistics of the measures as calculated on the whole collection of debates. Values obtained relying on Euclidean distance are included in Appendix B. Similarly to Garí Soler et al. (2022), we observe that measures that directly reflect similarity (OS_{TU}, SS_{TU} and SS_{TA}) have high values in a narrow range, due the anisotropy of BERT representations (Ethayarajh, 2019). For the same reason, measures that subtract two similarities ($sApp$ and $asApp$) have very low values. As expected in a debate setting, we find that other-similarity (OS_{TU}) is overall slightly lower than self-similarity measures (SS_{TU} and SS_{TA},

Measure	Avg	Min	Max	Std
SS_{TU}	0.71	0.63	0.75	0.02
OS_{TU}	0.69	0.62	0.72	0.02
SS_{TA}	0.70	0.61	0.75	0.02
$sApp$	0.01	-0.05	0.06	0.02
$asApp$	0.00	-0.04	0.05	0.01
DS	0.02	-0.25	0.34	0.11
SV	0.88	0.64	1.0	0.07

Table 2: Descriptive statistics of the proposed measures calculated on IQ2 with V_{t200} (or V_C for SV).

$p < 0.05$),[13] which indicates that a side's usage of a word tends to be more stable and coherent than usages across sides. The mean values of $sApp$ and $asApp$ are almost 0, suggesting that, on the whole, sides do not really tend to come closer to each other by the end of the debate in terms of word usage.

We also calculate the inter-correlations between our measures.[14] The only strong correlations found ($\rho > 0.5, p < 0.001$) are between SS_{TU} and SS_{TA} (0.93); and between $asApp$ and DS (0.77). This is not surprising, as these measures are related by definition. While each measure is contributing a specific kind of information, SS_{TA} could probably benefit from a different treatment of temporality. Correlations with Dialign measures are all weak ($\rho < 0.31$). This suggests that lexical and lexico-semantic alignment do not necessarily come together. This makes sense in a debate setting, where we expect semantic divergence on a very specific topic; but this result could be different in other types of conversations.

We compare the values of our asymmetric measures (SS_{TU}, SS_{TA}, $asApp$ and DS) when different sides win the debate. We use the 105 debates that do not end in a tie (52 where FOR wins, 53 where AGAINST wins).[15] We only find significant ($p < 0.05$) differences with the SS_{TA} measure. However, both $SS_{TA}(f)$ and $SS_{TA}(a)$ are overall slightly higher when AGAINST wins. Therefore, we cannot conclude that, when taken individually, the proposed measures reflect the winning side of a debate.

6 Toward Automatic Winner Prediction

We investigate whether the proposed measures can be used in combination in a supervised classification setting to automatically predict the winning side of a debate. For this experiment we again use the 105 debates where one side won. Given the little data available, we obtain model predictions in a leave-one-out setting. We fit a logistic regression model using different sets of features.

Measures	sim/dist	vocab.	Accuracy
asOurs	cos	V	**0.57**
asOurs	cos	V_{t200+C}	**0.57**
asOurs	eucl	V_{t200+C}	**0.57**
asOurs	eucl	V_{t200}	**0.57**
Ours	eucl	V_{t200}	**0.57**
asAll	cos	V_{t200+C}	0.54
asDia	-	-	0.52
Majority class baseline			0.50
Length baseline			0.49

Table 3: Results of different models on the winner prediction task. We include the best result obtained with each individual parameter.

Features We use three sets of asymmetric measures (calculated for each side): ours ($asOurs$), dialign measures ($asDia$), and all of them combined ($asAll$). Additionally, we try using our symmetric and asymmetric measures in combination ($Ours$). We experiment with different parameters when calculating our measures. We use cosine similarity (*cos*) or euclidean distance (*eucl*) and different vocabularies: everything (V) or words that are within the 200 words with highest tf-idf (V_{t200}), optionally in combination with V_C (V_{t200+C}).

Results Table 3 presents a summary of the results, in terms of accuracy, including the models that obtained the highest scores and at least one result (the best) for each parameter value. We also show the results of a majority class baseline that always predicts the class AGAINST (the most common in IQ2) as well as of a model that only relies on simple length-related features (*Length*).[16] The complete results can be found in Appendix B. Our asymmetric measures on their own obtain the best result (0.57) relying on different combinations of similarity or distance metrics and vocabularies. The same result is achieved with all our metrics calculated with Euclidean distance and V_{t200}. We do not observe a clear pattern as to the best similarity/distance or vocabulary to use. The combination of our measures with dialign or with our

[13]Determined with Mann Whitney U tests.

[14]We do not mix symmetric with asymmetric measures.

[15]We run t-tests or Mann Whitney U's tests according to normality, which is determined with Shapiro-Wilk tests.

[16]The following dialign measures: Num. utterances, num. tokens, % of tokens per side.

symmetric measures does not provide an advantage (0.54). Comparing to the best results obtained by the Dialign measures on their own (0.52), we conclude that asymmetric lexico-semantic measures are more useful for predicting a debate's winning side.

Most results are superior to the baselines, although not by a very large margin. This highlights both the importance of parameter optimization as well as the difficulty of the task. Predicting the winning side of a debate is hard, even for humans. Accuracy is below that obtained by Zhang et al. (2016) using conversational flow features in a similar setting (0.65). Overall, these results show that our asymmetric measures can, when used in combination, assist in (but not solve) this task.

7 Conclusion and Future Work

We have introduced and discussed the notion of lexico-semantic alignment. We have proposed a set of measures relying on contextualized word representations which are designed to account for different aspects of alignment, such as temporality and asymmetry. Our qualitative analysis shows that our metrics calculated with BERT reflect multiple semantic phenomena (e.g., collocations, connotation) that characterize the way each side of a debate uses specific words. We have also shown that the debate-level information provided by these metrics can be helpful for predicting a debate's winner.

In future work, we plan to study our measures' behavior on other kinds of conversations where the focus would be on individual speakers, such as task-oriented dialogs or everyday conversations involving multiple topics. We think that they are also potentially useful for detecting cases of misunderstanding due to lexical ambiguity or due to a language proficiency level mismatch between interlocutors. We can also refine our measures with a more fine-grained treatment of temporality and including information of the speaker who introduced each word. Finally, an obvious extension would be to experiment with different representations, e.g., from other language models.

Limitations

Coreference resolution quality. While we have taken care of choosing a good coreference solver and filtering out chains referring to speakers, the automatic resolution of coreference in dialog remains a challenging task. The quality of the tool has a direct impact on our SV measure, but also on our other estimations when including coreference chains.

The lack of manual annotation for lexico-semantic alignment makes it hard to run a systematic evaluation of the quality of the proposed measures. Our qualitative analysis provides valuable insight, but on one debate only. The classifier experiments demonstrate their usefulness for winner prediction, but they do not constitute an intrinsic evaluation. However, we note that annotating conversations with such information is bound to be a highly subjective, challenging and expensive task.

Acknowledgements

We thank Francesc Garí Soler for the interesting discussions, Shengjie Li for sharing the coreference resolution model, and the anonymous reviewers for their helpful comments and suggestions. This research is supported by the Télécom Paris research chair on Data Science and Artificial Intelligence for Digitalized Industry and Services (DSAIDIS) and by the Agence Nationale de la Recherche, REVITALISE project (ANR-21-CE33-0016).

References

Meghan J Babcock, Vivian P Ta, and William Ickes. 2014. Latent semantic similarity and language style matching in initial dyadic interactions. *Journal of Language and Social Psychology*, 33(1):78–88.

Holly P Branigan, Martin J Pickering, and Alexandra A Cleland. 2000. Syntactic co-ordination in dialogue. *Cognition*, 75(2):B13–B25.

Susan E Brennan and Herbert H Clark. 1996. Conceptual pacts and lexical choice in conversation. *Journal of experimental psychology: Learning, memory, and cognition*, 22(6):1482.

Jonathan P. Chang, Caleb Chiam, Liye Fu, Andrew Wang, Justine Zhang, and Cristian Danescu-Niculescu-Mizil. 2020. ConvoKit: A toolkit for the analysis of conversations. In *Proceedings of the 21th Annual Meeting of the Special Interest Group on Discourse and Dialogue*, pages 57–60, 1st virtual meeting. Association for Computational Linguistics.

Alexandra A Cleland and Martin J Pickering. 2003. The use of lexical and syntactic information in language production: Evidence from the priming of noun-phrase structure. *Journal of Memory and Language*, 49(2):214–230.

Frederick G Conrad and Michael F Schober. 2000. Clarifying question meaning in a household telephone survey. *Public opinion quarterly*, 64(1):1–28.

Cristian Danescu-Niculescu-Mizil, Lillian Lee, Bo Pang, and Jon Kleinberg. 2012. Echoes of power: Language effects and power differences in social interaction. In *Proceedings of the 21st international conference on World Wide Web*, pages 699–708.

Jacob Devlin, Ming-Wei Chang, Kenton Lee, and Kristina Toutanova. 2019. BERT: Pre-training of Deep Bidirectional Transformers for Language Understanding. In *Proceedings of the 2019 Conference of the North American Chapter of the Association for Computational Linguistics: Human Language Technologies, Volume 1 (Long and Short Papers)*, pages 4171–4186, Minneapolis, Minnesota. Association for Computational Linguistics.

Guillaume Dubuisson Duplessis, Caroline Langlet, Chloé Clavel, and Frédéric Landragin. 2021. Towards alignment strategies in human-agent interactions based on measures of lexical repetitions. *Language Resources and Evaluation*, 55:353–388.

Kawin Ethayarajh. 2019. How contextual are contextualized word representations? Comparing the geometry of BERT, ELMo, and GPT-2 embeddings. In *Proceedings of the 2019 Conference on Empirical Methods in Natural Language Processing and the 9th International Joint Conference on Natural Language Processing (EMNLP-IJCNLP)*, pages 55–65, Hong Kong, China. Association for Computational Linguistics.

Aina Garí Soler, Matthieu Labeau, and Chloé Clavel. 2022. One word, two sides: Traces of stance in contextualized word representations. In *Proceedings of the 29th International Conference on Computational Linguistics*, pages 3950–3959, Gyeongju, Republic of Korea. International Committee on Computational Linguistics.

Simon Garrod and Anthony Anderson. 1987. Saying what you mean in dialogue: A study in conceptual and semantic co-ordination. *Cognition*, 27(2):181–218.

Severin Laicher, Sinan Kurtyigit, Dominik Schlechtweg, Jonas Kuhn, and Sabine Schulte im Walde. 2021. Explaining and improving BERT performance on lexical semantic change detection. In *Proceedings of the 16th Conference of the European Chapter of the Association for Computational Linguistics: Student Research Workshop*, pages 192–202, Online. Association for Computational Linguistics.

Thomas K Landauer and Susan T Dumais. 1997. A Solution to Plato's Problem: The Latent Semantic Analysis Theory of Acquisition, Induction, and Representation of Knowledge. *Psychological review*, 104(2):211.

Shengjie Li, Hideo Kobayashi, and Vincent Ng. 2022. Neural anaphora resolution in dialogue revisited. In *Proceedings of the CODI-CRAC 2022 Shared Task on Anaphora, Bridging, and Discourse Deixis in Dialogue*, pages 32–47, Gyeongju, Republic of Korea. Association for Computational Linguistics.

Arthur B Markman and Valerie S Makin. 1998. Referential communication and category acquisition. *Journal of Experimental Psychology: General*, 127(4):331.

Ani Nenkova, Agustín Gravano, and Julia Hirschberg. 2008. High frequency word entrainment in spoken dialogue. In *Proceedings of ACL-08: HLT, Short Papers*, pages 169–172, Columbus, Ohio. Association for Computational Linguistics.

Jeffrey Pennington, Richard Socher, and Christopher Manning. 2014. Glove: Global Vectors for Word Representation. In *Proceedings of the 2014 Conference on Empirical Methods in Natural Language Processing (EMNLP)*, pages 1532–1543, Doha, Qatar. Association for Computational Linguistics.

Martin J Pickering and Simon Garrod. 2004. Toward a mechanistic psychology of dialogue. *Behavioral and brain sciences*, 27(2):169–190.

Vinodkumar Prabhakaran, Ashima Arora, and Owen Rambow. 2014. Staying on topic: An indicator of power in political debates. In *Proceedings of the 2014 Conference on Empirical Methods in Natural Language Processing (EMNLP)*, pages 1481–1486, Doha, Qatar. Association for Computational Linguistics.

David Reitter and Johanna D. Moore. 2007. Predicting success in dialogue. In *Proceedings of the 45th Annual Meeting of the Association of Computational Linguistics*, pages 808–815, Prague, Czech Republic. Association for Computational Linguistics.

Daniel Richardson, Rick Dale, and Kevin Shockley. 2008. Synchrony and swing in conversation: Coordination, temporal dynamics, and communication. *Embodied communication in humans and machines*, pages 75–94.

Daniel M Romero, Roderick I Swaab, Brian Uzzi, and Adam D Galinsky. 2015. Mimicry is presidential: Linguistic style matching in presidential debates and improved polling numbers. *Personality and Social Psychology Bulletin*, 41(10):1311–1319.

Michael F Schober. 2005. Conceptual Alignment in Conversation. *Other minds: How humans bridge the divide between self and others*, pages 239–252.

Kevin Shockley, Marie-Vee Santana, and Carol A Fowler. 2003. Mutual Interpersonal postural Constraints are Involved in Cooperative Conversation. *Journal of Experimental Psychology: Human Perception and Performance*, 29(2):326.

Arjen Stolk, Lennart Verhagen, and Ivan Toni. 2016. Conceptual Alignment: How Brains Achieve Mutual Understanding. *Trends in cognitive sciences*, 20(3):180–191.

Richard L Street Jr. 1984. Speech convergence and speech evaluation in fact-finding interviews. *Human Communication Research*, 11(2):139–169.

Vivian P Ta, Meghan J Babcock, and William Ickes. 2017. Developing Latent Semantic Similarity in Initial, Unstructured Interactions: The Words May Be All You Need. *Journal of Language and Social Psychology*, 36(2):143–166.

Scott R Vrana, Dylan T Vrana, Louis A Penner, Susan Eggly, Richard B Slatcher, and Nao Hagiwara. 2018. Latent Semantic Analysis: A new measure of patient-physician communication. *Social Science & Medicine*, 198:22–26.

Yang Xu. 2021. Global divergence and local convergence of utterance semantic representations in dialogue. In *Proceedings of the Society for Computation in Linguistics 2021*, pages 116–124, Online. Association for Computational Linguistics.

Yang Xu, Jeremy Cole, and David Reitter. 2018. Not that much power: Linguistic alignment is influenced more by low-level linguistic features rather than social power. In *Proceedings of the 56th Annual Meeting of the Association for Computational Linguistics (Volume 1: Long Papers)*, pages 601–610, Melbourne, Australia. Association for Computational Linguistics.

Juntao Yu, Sopan Khosla, Ramesh Manuvinakurike, Lori Levin, Vincent Ng, Massimo Poesio, Michael Strube, and Carolyn Rosé. 2022. The CODI-CRAC 2022 shared task on anaphora, bridging, and discourse deixis in dialogue. In *Proceedings of the CODI-CRAC 2022 Shared Task on Anaphora, Bridging, and Discourse Deixis in Dialogue*, pages 1–14, Gyeongju, Republic of Korea. Association for Computational Linguistics.

Justine Zhang, Ravi Kumar, Sujith Ravi, and Cristian Danescu-Niculescu-Mizil. 2016. Conversational flow in Oxford-style debates. In *Proceedings of the 2016 Conference of the North American Chapter of the Association for Computational Linguistics: Human Language Technologies*, pages 136–141, San Diego, California. Association for Computational Linguistics.

A Masking Experiment

We experiment with three different masking strategies: we replace the target word or phrase with a single [MASK] token (*one-mask*) or with as many [MASK] tokens as the original number of subwords (*multi-mask*) and compare these to the default approach of not masking (*no-mask*). The goal of masking is to abstract away from the surface form chosen by the speaker to refer to a concept, keeping only the meaning provided by the context in which it is used.

In order to find the best masking strategy to extract BERT representations for common words and concepts, we run a similar experiment to Garí Soler et al. (2022). Our evaluation criterion is the following: since we know that the two sides of a debate have opposing opinions, we want word representations found in one side to be more similar to each other than to representations from the other side. In other words, we expect the WITHIN-side similarity to be higher than the BETWEEN-side similarity. We verify which of the masking strategies yields representations that most clearly reflect the difference in opinion.

	no-mask	**one-mask**	**multi-mask**
V_W	**0.70**	0.69	0.69
V_C	**0.75**	0.71	0.71

Table 4: Accuracy of the three masking strategies with different kinds of shared vocabulary terms.

To obtain the data for a word w in a debate D, we randomly split the instances of a given side $I_{w,s}$ into two equally-sized sets of size ≥ 3, when possible. This results in four sentence sets (FOR$_1$, FOR$_2$, AGAINST$_1$, AGAINST$_2$). We obtain a word representation from each sentence set by averaging the contextualized representations of all word instances in it. With this data, we can run four comparisons: WITHIN-FOR, WITHIN-AGAINST, BETWEEN-1 (with FOR$_1$ and AGAINST$_1$,) and BETWEEN-2. We calculate the cosine similarity for each of these comparisons.

Accuracy is calculated as the proportion of (WITHIN, BETWEEN) comparison pairs (four per word) where the BETWEEN comparison had a lower similarity. Our experiments on V_W involve a total of 4,965 words (an average of 46 words per debate), which amount to 19,860 comparison pairs. For those on V_C, 841 concepts are used (an average of 7.8 per debate and a total of 3,364 comparison pairs).

Results are presented in Table 4 separately for common lemmas (V_W) and for concepts in coreference chains (V_C). Accuracy is higher in the *no-mask* setting, for both kinds of vocabulary elements, but particularly so for concepts found in coreference chains. We also note that accuracy is lower than in Garí Soler et al.'s 2022 experiments. This is not surprising, however, as they used sentences explicitly expressing a stance, while in debates not all sentences express an opinion unequivocally.

B Additional Tables and Figures

- Table 5: examples of words ranked by tf-idf.

Abolish the dead penalty
Top: penalty, death, abolish, parole, prison, punishment, deterrence, execution, sentence, victim...
Bottom: ...provide, learn, opening, university, week, city, work, open, power, turn

---

Global warming is not a crisis
Top: warming, climate, warm, temperature, greenhouse, crisis, atmosphere, dioxide, scientist, CO2...
Bottom: ...school, spend, friend, pay, set, week, city, everyone, view, lose

Table 5: Top and bottom noun and verb lemmas extracted from two debates ranked by tf-idf. Proper nouns are omitted.

- Table 6: examples of the coreference solver's output.
- Figure 2: illustration of the measures' behaviour on different toy examples.
- Table 7: descriptive statistics of our measures calculated with Euclidean distance.
- Table 8: Results of all tested settings on debate's winner prediction.

C Dialign Measures

We present below the list of Dialign measures (Dubuisson Duplessis et al., 2021) used in the paper. Note that the software finds matching lexical patterns in the conversation which can consist of multiple tokens; these are referred to as "expressions".

Symmetric (speaker-independent) measures:

- **Number of utterances**
- **Number of tokens**
- **Expression Lexicon Size (ELS)**† : number of established expressions in the dialog.
- **Expression Variety (EV)**† : variety of the shared expression lexicon.
- **Expression Repetition (ER)**† : proportion of tokens dedicated to repetitions.
- **Vocabulary overlap**† : ratio of shared vocabulary items.
- **ENTR**† : entropy of the lengths (in tokens) of shared expressions.
- **L**† : average length of shared expressions.
- **LMAX**† : maximum length of shared expressions.

The symmetric measures marked with † also have an asymmetric (speaker-dependent) version. Other asymmetric measures are:

- **Tokens (%)**
- **Initiated Expression**: ratio of shared expressions initiated by a speaker.

Debate title	Coreference examples
Obesity Is The Government's Business	We were also concerned about what was happening in **children**. For every **kid**, they get a report card that doesn't just give their arithmetic score.
	We cover some 8 percent of the **U.S.** work force for long term disability (...) (...) the surgeon of the general of the **United States** raised the alarm about (...) And **America** wouldn't be going broke.
Too Many Kids Go To College	(...) going to college is part of **the American dream** (...) We need to do better, and we can't give up on **the American dream**.
	(...) Students in the first tier system and a whole lot of **very expensive elite colleges** (...) (...) that is true of **the elite universities**.
The President Has Exceeded His Constitutional Authority by Waging War Without Congressional Authorization	(...) air strikes on **ISIS** (...) (...) the **Islamic State** didn't exist in 2001 (...) (...) **it** has distanced **itself** from the core al-Qaeda leadership (...)

Table 6: Examples of the coreference solver's output for different debates. We find coreference chains containing synonyms, phrases, paraphrases and pronouns.

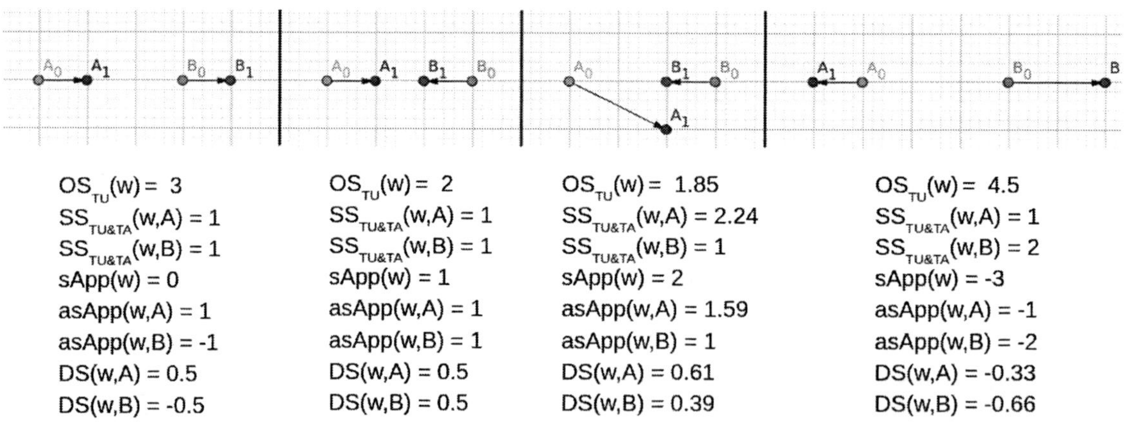

$OS_{TU}(w) = 3$	$OS_{TU}(w) = 2$	$OS_{TU}(w) = 1.85$	$OS_{TU}(w) = 4.5$
$SS_{TU\&TA}(w,A) = 1$	$SS_{TU\&TA}(w,A) = 1$	$SS_{TU\&TA}(w,A) = 2.24$	$SS_{TU\&TA}(w,A) = 1$
$SS_{TU\&TA}(w,B) = 1$	$SS_{TU\&TA}(w,B) = 1$	$SS_{TU\&TA}(w,B) = 1$	$SS_{TU\&TA}(w,B) = 2$
sApp(w) = 0	sApp(w) = 1	sApp(w) = 2	sApp(w) = -3
asApp(w,A) = 1	asApp(w,A) = 1	asApp(w,A) = 1.59	asApp(w,A) = -1
asApp(w,B) = -1	asApp(w,B) = 1	asApp(w,B) = 1	asApp(w,B) = -2
DS(w,A) = 0.5	DS(w,A) = 0.5	DS(w,A) = 0.61	DS(w,A) = -0.33
DS(w,B) = -0.5	DS(w,B) = 0.5	DS(w,B) = 0.39	DS(w,B) = -0.66

Figure 2: Values obtained with each measure in different toy situations. For ease of interpretation, we calculate the measures with Euclidean distance. Values of SS_{TU}, SS_{TA} and OS_{TU} are to be interpreted as distances. The sign in measures that rely on similarity differences ($sApp$, $asApp$, DS) has been adapted so a negative value indicates distancing. A and B represent the two sides of a debate, and subscripts 0 and 1 refer to the two time steps. In such simplified setting, with only two instances per side, SS_{TU} and SS_{TA} are equivalent.

Measure	Avg	Min	Max	Std
SS_{TU}	14.92	13.29	17.37	0.64
OS_{TU}	15.52	14.33	17.52	0.56
SS_{TA}	15.29	13.74	17.83	0.66
$sApp$	0.167	-1.51	1.58	0.45
$asApp$	0.00	-1.16	1.03	0.32
DS	0.01	-0.23	0.32	0.12

Table 7: Descriptive statistics of the proposed measures calculated on IQ2 using Euclidean distance and V_{t200}.

Measures	sim/dist	vocab.	Accuracy
asOurs	cos	V	**0.57**
asOurs	cos	V_{t200+C}	**0.57**
asOurs	eucl	V_{t200+C}	**0.57**
asOurs	eucl	V_{t200}	**0.57**
Ours	eucl	V_{t200}	**0.57**
Ours	cos	V_{t200}	0.55
asOurs	cos	V_{t200}	0.54
asAll	cos	V_{t200+C}	0.54
Ours	eucl	V_{t200+C}	0.54
asAll	eucl	V_{t200+C}	0.54
asDia	-	-	0.52
asAll	cos	V	0.52
asOurs	eucl	V	0.52
asAll	eucl	V	0.52
asAll	eucl	V_{t200}	0.51
Ours	cos	V_{t200+C}	0.50
asAll	cos	V_{t200}	0.50
Ours	cos	V	0.49
Ours	eucl	V	0.47
Majority class baseline			0.50
Length baseline			0.49

Table 8: Complete results on the debate's winner prediction task.

Exploring Linguistic Style Matching in Online Communities: The Role of Social Context and Conversation Dynamics

Aparna Ananthasubramaniam*, Hong Chen*, Jason Yan*, Kenan Alkiek*, Jiaxin Pei*, Agrima Seth*, Lavinia Dunagan*, Minje Choi*, Benjamin Litterer* and **David Jurgens**
School of Information, University of Michigan
{akananth,hongcc,jasonyan,kalkiek,pedropei, agrima,laviniad,minje,blitt,jurgens}@umich.edu

Abstract

Linguistic style matching (LSM) in conversations can be reflective of several aspects of social influence such as power or persuasion. However, how LSM relates to the outcomes of online communication on platforms such as Reddit is an unknown question. In this study, we analyze a large corpus of two-party conversation threads in Reddit where we identify all occurrences of LSM using two types of style: the use of function words and formality. Using this framework, we examine how levels of LSM differ in conversations depending on several social factors within Reddit: post and subreddit features, conversation depth, user tenure, and the controversiality of a comment. Finally, we measure the change of LSM following loss of status after community banning. Our findings reveal the interplay of LSM in Reddit conversations with several community metrics, suggesting the importance of understanding conversation engagement when understanding community dynamics.

1 Introduction

Social influence can be subtle. When two persons converse, their interpersonal dynamics can lead to one person adopting the language of the other. For example, in settings where one person has higher status or power, the lower-status person may unconsciously begin mirroring the language of the other (Danescu-Niculescu-Mizil et al., 2012). This process has been described as *accommodation* (Giles et al., 2007) or *linguistic style matching (LSM)* (Niederhoffer and Pennebaker, 2002) and can reflect the underlying influence that individuals have on each other (Chartrand and Bargh, 1999). Past work has primarily focused on how linguistic influence changes relative to the identities of the speakers. However, the larger social context in which a conversation happens also plays a role in determining whether an individual may be influential. Here, we perform a large-scale study of linguistic influence to test how specific types of social context influence the level of accommodation.

Past work in the social sciences has studied accommodation to understand the influence and social power dynamics in specific settings, like job interviews (applicants and interviewers) (Willemyns et al., 1997) and academic context (students and faculty)(Jones et al., 1999). Also, LSM has been studied to understand group dynamics (Gonzales et al., 2010) and negotiations (Ireland and Henderson, 2014). Work in NLP has operationalized these theories to test accommodation theory in new domains. Typically, these works adopt some tests for measuring influence in language and have shown these measures correlate with known social differences. However, it is yet unknown how LSM occurs in conversations in online community platforms and differs by community dynamics.

Our work examines the larger context in which linguistic influence occurs. Using a large sample of 2.3 million conversations from Reddit and two measures of linguistic influence, we test how the level of linguistic influence correlates with conversational outcomes, such as conversation length and even the continued presence of a person in a community. Further, we examine how specific social and contextual factors influence the rates of linguistic influence. For instance, we discover that the controversy level of the parent comment can lead to different dynamics of style matching in the conversation threads.

This paper offers the following three contributions. First, we systematically compare complementary measures of accommodation, showing clear evidence of style accommodation in Reddit conversations. Second, we draw the relationships of several social factors that affect LSM, including levels of engagement, the popularity of the content, and tenure within a subreddit. Third, we demon-

*denotes equal contribution

Proceedings of the First Workshop on Social Influence in Conversations (SICon 2023), pages 64–74
July 14, 2023

strate the use of LSM to measure the loss of status through the banning of subreddits. We have released all code and data for full reproducibility.[1]

2 Accommodation and its Measurement

In this section, we discuss communication accommodation theory and associated sociolinguistic research to outline the accommodation of communicative behavior based on perceived social power dynamics. Subsequently, we explore the concept of linguistic style matching and methods adopted by researchers to quantify this phenomenon. We also investigate various factors that contribute to LSM variations and their strategic uses.

2.1 Accommodation Theory as Social Influence

When two individuals engage in social interaction, they may either converge or diverge in their communicative behavior. The Communication Accommodation Theory (CAT) suggests that the degree of convergence or divergence is affected by the relative social power between the interlocutors (Xu et al., 2018). Asymmetric convergence is more likely to occur in situations where there is a power imbalance between the interlocutors. Individuals with lower social power or status are more likely to adapt their communication style to align with those in higher or dominant positions (Muir et al., 2016). For instance, Puerto Ricans in New York City during the 1970s, who were perceived to hold less power than African Americans, adopted the dialect of African Americans to converge with their more powerful counterparts (Wolfram, 1974).

Social power has been often found to be an important determinant of degrees of accommodation (Giles et al., 1991; Ng and Bradac, 1993) and interactants of differential social power or social status can act in a complementary fashion (Street, 1991).

2.2 Linguistic Style Matching

Linguistic alignment is a pervasive phenomenon that occurs in human communication where interactants unconsciously coordinate their language usage. This coordination, described as convergence in the psycholinguistic theory of communication accommodation, involves aspects such as word choice, syntax, utterance length, pitch, and gestures (Giles et al., 1991). Linguistic style matching (LSM) is a specific manifestation of linguistic alignment, wherein individuals unconsciously match their speaking or writing styles during conversations (Ireland et al., 2011). Unlike content accommodation, LSM focuses on stylistic accommodation, examining how things are communicated rather than what they communicate.

Individuals strategically negotiate their language style to decrease social distance, seek approval, and accommodate each other. LSM can also reflect the level of common understanding and conceptualization of the conversation topic between speakers. The degree of LSM can indicate social power dynamics as indicated by (Giles et al., 2007). Empirical evidence from recent studies (Danescu-Niculescu-Mizil et al., 2012) showed that participants with less power (such as lawyers or non-administrative roles in Wikipedia) exhibit greater coordination in conversational behavior than participants with high power (such as justices or administrators). Additionally, Noble and Fernández (2015) identified a positive correlation between linguistic accommodation and social network centrality, which effect can be greater than the effect of power status distinction. Studies by Muir et al. (2016, 2017) further show that individuals in a lower position of power tend to accommodate their linguistic style to match that of their higher-power counterparts during face-to-face communication as well as computer-mediated communication.

The variance in LSM can be attributed to various social and psychological factors and can be triggered for different purposes. Linguistic alignment may signal likability and agreement, relate to seeking approval or arise from social desirability. Higher levels of accommodation in social behaviors are found to be associated with increased feelings of affiliation, liking, and successful interpersonal relationships (Bayram and Ta, 2019). Thus, linguistic alignment can be strategically employed to establish relationship initiation and stability (Ireland et al., 2011), increase group cohesion, and task performance (Gonzales et al., 2010), and assist in negotiations (Taylor and Thomas, 2008). Furthermore, alignment has been found to enhance persuasiveness, motivating listeners to adopt healthier practices (Cialdini, 2001) while in some cases like presidential debates, it has been perceived as more aggressive (Romero et al., 2015). The degree of matching may differ based on context and individual factors.

[1] https://github.com/davidjurgens/style-influence

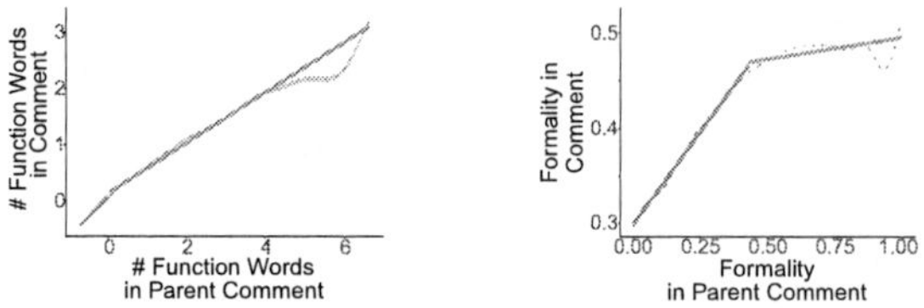

(a) Accommodation, # Function Words

(b) Accommodation, Formality

Figure 1: Commenters on Reddit accommodate to the (a) # function words and b) formality of the comment they are replying to. Typically, the level of accommodation is higher when responding to posts with below-average (red) than above-average (blue) style.

3 Data

Reddit is a popular social media platform with a forum-based interface. It allows users to interact with dispersed individuals who share similar experiences or topics of interest. Our dataset to study LSM spans from July 2019 to December 2022 and includes 35M users and 500K subreddits.

Using the Pushshift Reddit Dataset which contains the full history of comments aggregated on a monthly basis (Baumgartner et al., 2020), we construct conversation threads from the comments and filter those that satisfy the following conditions: (1) the conversation chain consists of exactly two users; (2) the beginning of the conversation chain must be a root comment which does not have a parent comment; and (3) the lengths of a conversation chain must between 3 and 100. These conditions allow us to capture conversation dynamics between exactly two users without any interference. Our resulting dataset contains 16,893,013 conversation turns (or comments) across 2,305,775 conversation chains from 68,788 subreddits.

4 How should we measure linguistic influence?

Computational work has proposed multiple approaches for both what to measure and how to measure linguistic influence. In this section, we aim to build intuition for what the two measures of accommodation—using function words and formality—are operationalizing.

4.1 Linguistic Style Markers

Our study measures linguistic influence with two complementary style markers. We use the notation m to refer to a marker throughout.

Marker 1: Function Words Function words (e.g. pronouns, prepositions, articles, and auxiliary words) are primarily employed unconsciously and frequently and incorporate social knowledge for comprehension and usage (Meyer and Bock, 1999; Ireland and Pennebaker, 2010). Prior computational studies of linguistic accommodation have measured linguistic influence by tracking the relative frequencies of function words across conversation turns (Danescu-Niculescu-Mizil et al., 2011; Babcock et al., 2014; Gonzales et al., 2010). Function words reflect *how* content is expressed, rather than what specific content is expressed (e.g., content words) and are thought to be a better proxy for unconscious language processing (Tausczik and Pennebaker, 2010). Here, we use the function words defined by the Linguistic Inquiry and Word Count (LIWC) lexicon (Pennebaker et al., 2001; Pennebaker and Chung, 2007).

Marker 2: Formality Individuals adopt a specific register that is appropriate to their position in the social context, real or desired (Niederhoffer and Pennebaker, 2002). A commonly varied register is the level of formality used when speaking to another. The level of formality shown by a speaker is known to reflect the speaker's opinion towards a topic or their closeness to the listener (Hovy, 1987). Unlike function words, variation in formality often requires conscious processing to select the appropriate phrasing in a given circumstance. As a result, it offers a complementary view into how a speaker influences another through shifting the conversation towards a more formal or informal register.

Here, we measure formality using a supervised classification model. The model is a fine-tuned RoBERTa-based classifier (Liu et al., 2019) trained on the GYAFC (Rao and Tetreault, 2018) and Online Formality Corpus (Pavlick and Tetreault, 2016) datasets; we use the model available from the Hugging Face API[2]. Both datasets contain social media text and the reported model performance is high for both blogs and Q&A text (Spearman's ρ>0.7). Using this classifier, each comment's formality is measured on a continuous scale in [0,1].

Importantly, these style variables are related; function word frequency also changes in more formal contexts, where articles and prepositions typically become more common while pronouns and interjections become less common (Heylighen and

[2] `https://huggingface.co/s-nlp/roberta-base-formality-ranker`

Dewaele, 1999). Content word-based measures of style and function word counts are thought to capture the same latent style variables, i.e., they are interchangeable at a stylometric level (Grieve, 2023).

4.2 Measuring Linguistic Influence

At a high-level, linguistic influence (also referred to as LSM or accommodation in this paper) is measured by testing whether the value for some measure m of a comment made by user a is predictive of the value of m in the reply to that comment by user b. Therefore, one straightforward way to measure accommodation is with linear regression: $m_b \sim \beta_0 + \beta_1 m_a$ where β_0 reflects the baseline level of the measure (e.g., the average formality) and β_1 measures the level of accommodation (e.g., the average increase in formality associated with a 1-unit increase in the formality of the parent comment). However, as Xu et al. (2018) note, the characteristics of a comment are likely influenced by other unrelated factors such as the length of the comment or the number of turns in the conversation. Indeed, they show that unless one controls for such factors, linguistic influence may be overestimated. Therefore, we used a mixed-effects regression to control for comment a and b's length in tokens (fixed effects L_a, L_b), the number of replies $r_{b \to a}$ that b has made to a so far in the conversation. To capture individual and community-level variation, we include random effects to control for the effect of the subreddit s; these random effects let us control for differences in the norms of communities (e.g., some communities are more/less formal) to test for relative changes in m. Linguistic accommodation is modeled as

$$m_b \sim \beta_0 + \beta_1 m_a + \\ \beta_2 L_a + \beta_3 L_b + \beta_4 r_{b \to a} + (1|s)$$

where β_1 measures the level of accommodation.

4.3 Results

We first observe clear evidence of accommodation in both style markers: parent comments with more function words receive replies with more function words (Figure 1a), and more formal parent comments receive more formal replies (Figure 1b). For comments where we have the text of the original post, we observe accommodation even after controlling for the author and original post's style markers, suggesting that users may accommodate to the style of the person they are interacting with in the comment thread. However, this effect plateaus when the parent comment has above-average levels of a style marker, suggesting a potential threshold for the impact of parent comment style on reply style. This attenuation of effect may be the result of several mechanisms, including regression to the mean or an author modulating their replies according to their own personal style (i.e., a more extreme parent comment may trigger greater modulation).

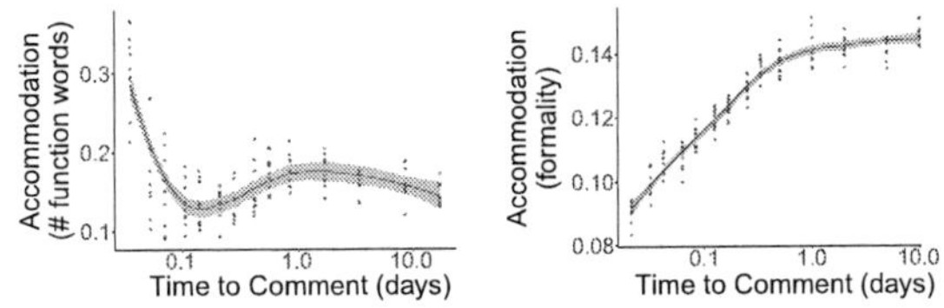

(a) Time to Comment, # Function Words (b) Time to Comment, Formality

Figure 2: Commenters on Reddit are more likely to accommodate (a) # function words when they reply quickly (suggesting subconscious accommodation) and b) formality of the comment when they reply slowly (suggesting strategic accommodation).

Second, the two style markers are almost perfectly uncorrelated, suggesting that they measure distinct constructs. In order to calculate the correlation between these two measures, we randomly sample 1,000 subsets of the conversation turns and calculate the extent of accommodation in function words and formality in that subset. The correlation between the function-word- and formality-based accommodation scores is -0.00171.

Third, accommodation in the two style markers seems to occur via fundamentally distinct psychological processes. Accommodation can occur either 1) through a subconscious priming mechanism, where the speaker instinctively repeats what they hear; or 2) through a more conscious, strategic act with communicative intent (Doyle and Frank, 2016). Figure 2 suggests that function-word-accommodation seems to be an unconscious form of relating to the audience, while formality-accommodation seems to be more intentional and strategic. Commenters exhibit greater accommodation in function words when they take less time to reply to the prior comment (2a) and greater accommodation in formality when they reply more slowly (2b). These results are consistent with prior work, suggesting that accommodation of function words occurs subconsciously (reflexively, takes less time) and builds on this work to show that accommoda-

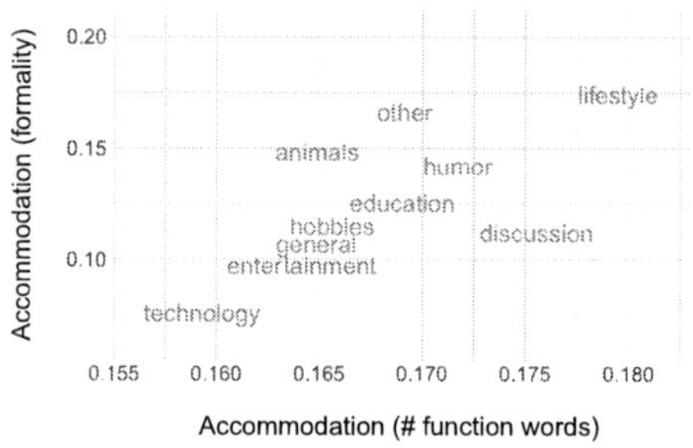

Figure 3: Level of accommodation in the number of function words (x-axis) and in formality (y-axis).

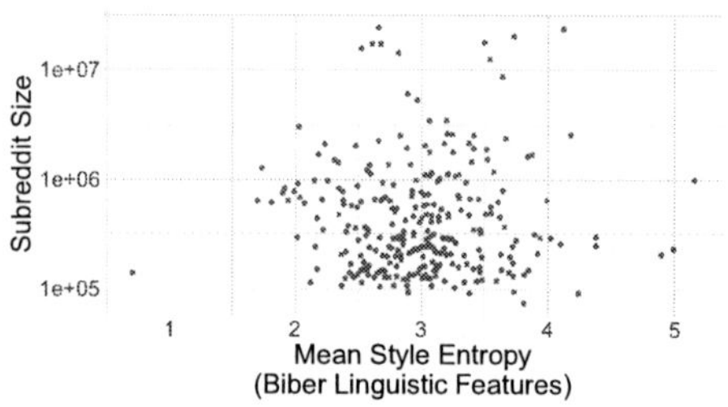

Figure 4: The mean Shannon Entropy of Biber's linguistic features (x-axis) is uncorrelated to the subreddit's number of subscribers (y-axis) ($p = 0.41$). Entropy is calculated using a random sample of comments in each subreddit.

tion in other style markers, like formality, occurs strategically (intentionally, takes more time).

Fourth, there is little variation in accommodation across subreddit characteristics. Figure 3 shows the levels of accommodation across ten different types of subreddits, using an existing taxonomy of popular subreddits.[3] While certain types of subreddits (e.g., lifestyle) tend to have higher levels of accommodation than others (e.g., technology, entertainment), most differences are only weakly significant ($p > 0.01$) with a small effect size. Moreover, Figure 4 shows the relationship between subreddit size and variation in linguistic style, for 300 subreddits sampled based on their number of subscribers. To calculate variation in linguistic style, we use Biber (1988)'s comprehensive set of linguistic features. Linguistic variation within each subreddit is estimated as the mean Shannon Entropy of each Biber tag frequency at the subreddit level. Despite expectations that larger communities may exhibit greater diversity in language use (Kocab et al., 2019), we find no relationship between community size and linguistic variation.

[3] https://www.reddit.com/r/ListOfSubreddits/wiki/listofsubreddits/

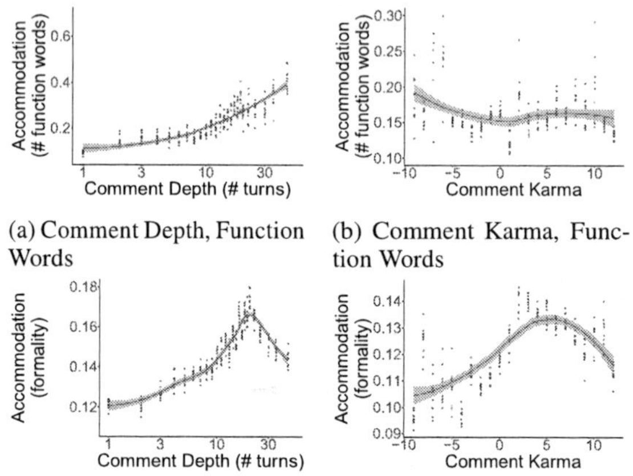

(a) Comment Depth, Function Words
(b) Comment Karma, Function Words
(c) Comment Depth, Formality
(d) Comment Karma, Formality

Figure 5: Characteristics of the comment are non-linearly associated with accommodation, including comment depth (a,c) and comment karma (b,d).

Overall, these findings point to the nuanced dynamics of LSM in online interactions, indicating that factors such as function word usage and formality in the parent comment are associated with the linguistic style and tone of replies.

5 What factors about a comment influence the degree of accommodation?

LSM can be affected by many factors and existing studies have pointed out the roles of not only linguistic characteristics but also the contextual factors affecting LSM (Niederhoffer and Pennebaker, 2002). In this section, we study the connection between LSM and a series of contextual factors where the comment is posted (i.e., comment depth) and the "success" of a comment (i.e., comment Karma and parent comment Karma).

5.1 Experimental Setup

To test for heterogeneity in the level of accommodation with respect to several covariates (e.g., depth, Karma), we run a mixed effects regression similar to Section 4.2, but include an interaction term to test whether accommodation changes significantly with respect to some covariate (say, Karma K):

$$m_b \sim \beta_0 + \beta_1 m_a + \beta_2 K + \beta_3 m_a * K + \beta_4 L_a + \beta_5 L_b + \beta_6 r_{b \to a} + (1|b) + (1|s)$$

Here, β_1 measures the level of accommodation when $K = 0$ and β_3 measures the increase in accommodation when K increases by one point; if β_3

is significantly different from 0, then we have evidence that accommodation is heterogeneous with respect to Karma.

In order to visualize these effects, we fit the model in the above equation to estimate accommodation at different values of Karma. In order to appropriately represent uncertainty in this model, we sample 100,000 conversation turns at each value of Karma 10 times and use this to obtain 10 different estimates of accommodation for each value of the covariate. To visualize the association between Karma and accommodation, we plot Karma on the x-axis and the LSM estimates on the y-axis.

5.2 Results

As shown in Figure 5, various factors of comments are related to LSM.

Comment depth Comment depth reflects the position of a comment in the conversation tree. Deeper comments are usually posted in longer conversations and when the users are more engaged in the dialogue. As shown in Figure 5a and Figure 5c, comment depth is positively correlated with LSM. However, accommodation in formality drops off for very deep comments. LSM happen more when the comment is deeper in the conversation tree, suggesting that users tend to match not only the content but also the structural aspects of their language in response to their interlocutor. Such a trend could be due to greater investment in the conversation. When two users are involved in longer and deeper conversations, they are more likely to be engaged in the conversation, which may lead to higher subconscious but lower conscious LSM.

Comment Karma A key feature of Reddit is the ability for users to upvote or downvote comments, which determines the comment's karma - a measure of its popularity within the community. In figure 5, we observe several non-linear associations between karma, comment characteristics, and LSM. In terms of comment karma, users' LSM tends to remain relatively constant, except for cases where the comment has very high karma, which is associated with an increase in LSM. This finding implies that highly popular comments may foster greater linguistic alignment between users.

We also see that comments with low karma have lower levels of LSM than comments with high karma (Figure 5d), which makes sense since we'd expect users to respond better to comments whether the author is mirroring their interlocutor. Notably, this upward trend reverses in comments with very high karma – which have lower levels of LSM than comments with lower levels of karma. The reversal of the LSM trend in comments with high karma warrants further exploration. One possible explanation for this phenomenon is that highly upvoted comments may exhibit unconventional linguistic styles that deviate from the norm, which could be seen as novel by the Reddit community. Another explanation may be that comments with high karma are more likely to be popular in larger, diverse communities where users may have a wider range of linguistic styles. Additionally, it is possible that comments with high karma receive a higher volume of comments and interactions, which may dilute the overall LSM score due to the presence of diverse linguistic styles from multiple interlocutors.

6 What effect does accommodation have on the conversation itself?

Linguistic accommodation is usually associated with positive social benefits (Taylor and Thomas, 2008; Gonzales et al., 2010). Here, we test whether linguistic accommodation is associated with two positive behaviors in social media: sustained conversation and length of participation in a subreddit.

6.1 Experimental Setup

We fit a linear regression on conversational dyads following the LSM measure in Section 4.2. Following the procedure from the prior section, we estimate the level of accommodation for comments around a particular covariate by sampling 100,000 conversation turns at or near the respective value of the covariate. Once again, we verify that differences between covariates are significant, by introducing interaction terms in the regression and testing for a statistically significance effect.

6.2 Results

Figures 6a and 6b compare the effect of alignment when conditioned on the total length of the conversation thread. For both functions words and formality, we observe from the fitted lines that accommodation is more likely to happen from longer conversations, but only up to a certain length of approximately 30-40. This suggests the possibility of LSM being an earlier indicator of how engaged the users will be in a conversation. On the other hand, the likelihood of accommodation in formality decreases when the conversation becomes longer

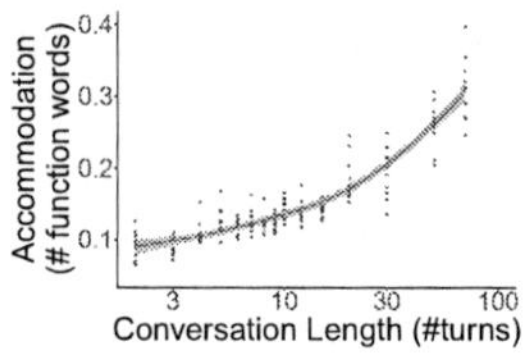

(a) Length, # Function Words

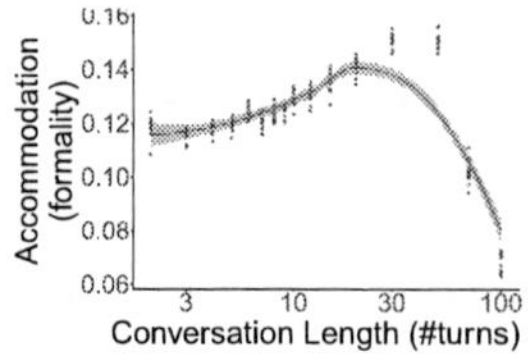

(b) Length, Formality

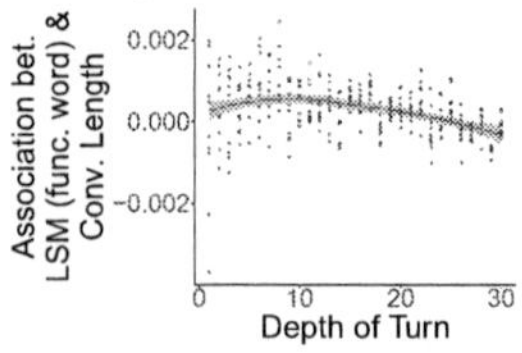

(c) Depth x Length, # Function Words

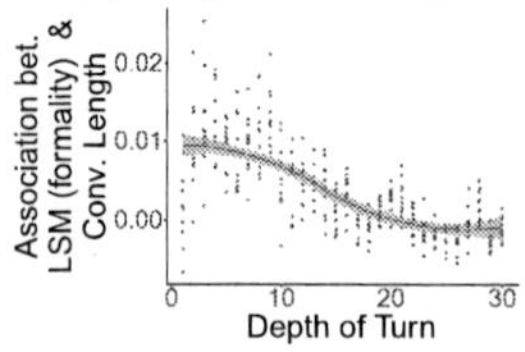

(d) Depth x Length, Formality

Figure 6: The number of turns in a conversation is associated with the level of accommodation in each turn: (a-b) Longer conversations (i.e., threads consisting of more conversation turns) are associated with higher accommodation, up to a threshold; for sufficiently long conversations, the association is negative for formality. (c-d) The effect of alignment on conversation length is stronger earlier in the conversation and weaker as more conversational turns occur.

than a certain threshold, which suggests that speakers may stop consciously trying to accommodate once the conversation becomes sufficiently long.

Figures 6c and 6d compare accommodation likelihoods at a given turn within a conversation. Interestingly, we can observe that LSM starts off highest at the beginning of a conversation and decreases as the number of turns increases. Combining the two results, we can conjecture that while the degree of LSM generally decreases within a conversation thread, the initial levels of LSM observed at the early stages of a conversation can indicate how engaged the speakers will be, which one can use to estimate the overall conversation length.

How does LSM differ by tenure and number of subsequent posts in a subreddit? Figure 7 shows that, for both style markers, users who have a longer tenure in the subreddit or who post more in the subreddit in the next month tend to display higher subconscious and lower conscious LSM. We consider these results as evidence of the "lifespan" of a user's engagement toward conversations held within that subreddit, and ultimately engagement toward the subreddit itself, which has been noted in prior work (Danescu-Niculescu-Mizil et al., 2013).

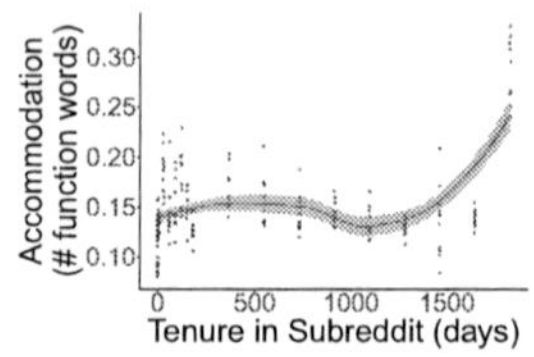

(a) Tenure, # Function Words

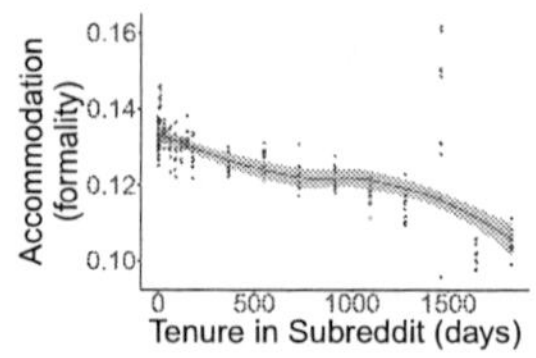

(b) Tenure, Formality

Figure 7: Alignment is associated with engagement: (a) stronger function-word LSM and (b) weaker formality LSM for higher tenure in subreddit.

7 What effect does the social context have on accommodation: Controversiality?

In this section, we examine whether LSM differs by social contexts that arise during conversations. Specifically, we focus on the controversy level of the parent comment. In contrast to non-controversial issues, controversial issues lead to competitive disagreement, where the goal of the groups involved in argumentation is to convince the opponent group(s) of the validity of one's point of view (Ilie, 2021). The arguments on controversial issues tend to invite strong emotions with negative affect (Mejova et al., 2014) and deteriorate the deliberation in the public sphere because interactions often turn uncivil (Doxtader, 1991).

7.1 Experimental Setup

Following the procedure from the prior section, we estimate the level of accommodation for comments at each covariate, separately for controversial and non-controversial comments. When a comment or post receives a substantial number of upvotes and downvotes, Reddit automatically designates it as controversial. The exact method used by Reddit to determine controversy remains private. However, the Reddit API offers a binary label indicating whether a comment is controversial or non-controversial (Koncar et al., 2021). Approximately 1.30% (n=218,899) of the comments in our sample are labeled as controversial.

We test that differences between conditions are significant with a three-way interaction term in the regression between the parent-comment style, the comment's Karma (or other covariates) and the comment's controversiality: $m_a \times K \times C$.

7.2 Results

Figure 8 reveals that LSM occurs differently in controversial and non-controversial comments. For both function words and formality, LSM is less

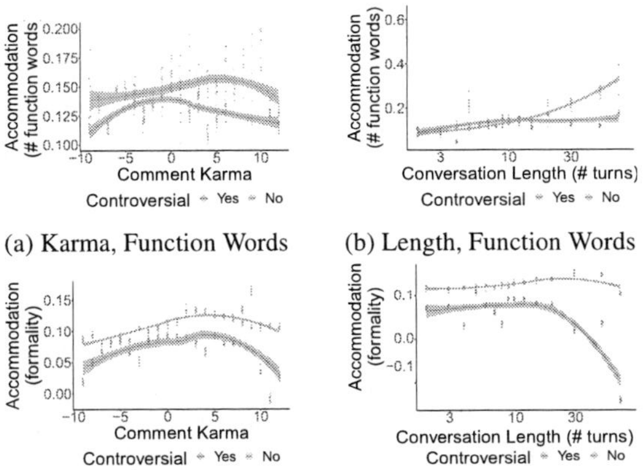

(a) Karma, Function Words

(b) Length, Function Words

(c) Karma, Formality

(d) Length, Formality

Figure 8: The associations between LSM and "success" are very different for controversial (red line) and non-controversial (blue line) comments: (a) Very-high-karma controversial comments tend to have lower, rather than higher, function-word alignment; and (c) overall lower formality-alignment. (b) Compared to shorter threads, longer controversial threads tend to have lower, rather than higher, function-word alignment and (d) formality alignment.

likely to occur in controversial rather than non-controversial comments when the conversation length is below a certain threshold (12-14). Interestingly, we see that this trend is strengthened as the conversation length increases. One possible explanation is that controversial comments generate more initial interest that promotes users to engage more in conversations. However, this initial effect is washed away as the conversation takes further turns, and the conversation is less likely to continue due to reasons such as incivility. Non-controversial comments, on the other hand, enjoy less of this initial boost and is more likely to carry on if the users have accommodated each other's language during their conversation.

With the addition of Karma, we can observe a more complex trend that plays out differently for each style marker. For function words, conversations in controversial comments have a nonlinear relationship that drops as the parent comment's Karma increases, whereas a weak positive correlation can be observed for non-controversial comments and levels of Karma. In contrast, for formality, LSM occurs most at comments with about 0-5 Karma and decreases for higher Karma for both controversial and non-controversial comments.

Overall, we observe that social contexts that are defined by the community platform such as Karma or controversy have complex, nonlinear effects on how LSM occurs in conversations.

8 Loss of Status via Community Banning

Reddit bans specific subreddit communities as a result of policy violations, such as repeated posting of highly offensive content or lack of moderator oversight (Chandrasekharan et al., 2017). When users are highly active in such communities, the ban potentially results in a loss of status, as they are forced to find new communities to participate in. Here, we test the extent to which users change how they are linguistically influenced by others after such a ban. While prior work has studied how users change after *gaining* status (e.g., Danescu-Niculescu-Mizil et al., 2012), our unique setting allows us to perform a novel study of the potentially humbling effects of status loss. In addition, a study of the subreddit `r/changemyview` suggests that formality is (weakly) associated with more effective persuasion on Reddit (Dayter and Messerli, 2022); we hypothesize that users who recently experienced a ban may have multiple pragmatic reasons to accommodate more.

8.1 Experimental Setup

We test for changes to linguistic influence using a pseudo-causal difference-in-difference analysis (Lechner et al., 2011). Subreddit ban dates were determined by identifying all banned subreddits and then using the last date of a post in that subreddit. Our sample includes 1,024 subreddits banned between July 2019 and December 2022. We identify 16,686 users in our sample who made at least one comment in these subreddits in the 30 days before their ban. Each user from a banned subreddit is considered as treated and matched with a control user who did not participate in that subreddit.

Three analyses of the effect of the ban are performed, controlling for user-level and temporal factors. First, we estimate the effect of commenting in a banned subreddit, by comparing posts made in banned subreddits t months before the ban to posts made by the same users at the same time, in other subreddits. Second, using a difference-in-differences approach, we estimate the effect of banning a subreddit on authors' use of accommodation in (unbanned) subreddits they were active in for t months before and after the ban. This second analysis measures the spill-over effects of the ban on users' behaviors in other subreddits; the

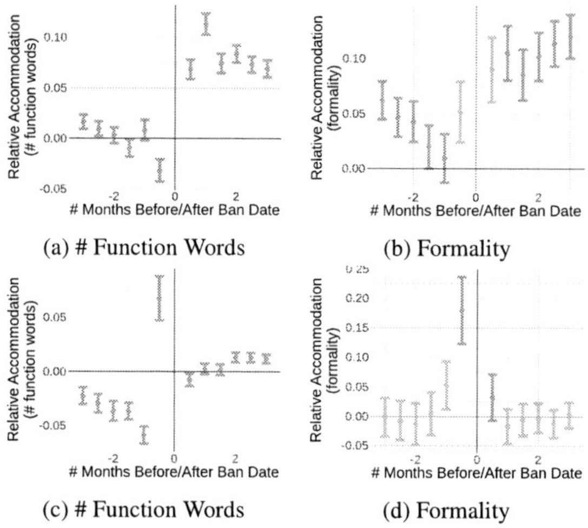

Figure 9: When a subreddit is banned, (a,c) users who commented there tend to have higher LSM in other subreddits, (b) users tend to have higher LSM in function words in subreddits they migrate to, (d) LSM in formality tends to temporarily increases just before the subreddit is banned then returns to near-baseline levels in subreddits they migrate to.

difference-in-differences estimator uses users active in these subreddits at the same time, but not in a banned subreddit, as a control for temporal and subreddit-level effects. Third, we calculate the effect of the ban on commenting behavior in subreddits users migrated to (i.e., newly joined) after the ban was enacted. The difference-in-differences estimator compares accommodation in comments in the banned subreddits to comments in the subreddits these users migrated to; to isolate the effect of migration, the difference between the comments in the migrated and banned subreddits are compared against the spill-over effects in other subreddits that users were a part of during this time.

8.2 Results

Our results suggest that policy actions on Reddit, such as banning, have an effect on the level of accommodation by users. First, the level of subconscious accommodation tends to be lower in banned subreddits than other subreddits the users comment in during the 30 days before the ban (the effects are all below 0 in Figure 9c ($p < 2e - 16$).

Second, following the banning of a subreddit, users tend to change their LSM levels in other subreddits: Figure 9 shows that function-word-mirroring (Figure 9a) and formality-mirroring (Figure 9b) increase after a subreddit is banned. Our results suggest that users who had previously been active in banned subreddits may have been making an effort to index agreeableness by accommodating (e.g., to avoid losing status in another community).

Third, changes in accommodation are initially amplified in subreddits that these users migrate to after their original community was banned. The comments left by these users in banned subreddits exhibit higher levels of accommodation than would be expected immediately before the ban and maintain higher subconscious accommodation in subreddits they migrated (Figures 9c and 9d$p < 2e - 16$). Since function-word mirroring is likely subconscious and formality-mirroring strategic (Section 4), our results suggest that users who had previously been active in banned subreddits may have, intrinsically, indexed agreeableness by accommodating (e.g., to gain status in their new community) but without making a conscious effort (e.g., because they were upset about the loss of a status). These users also increased LSM in the subreddit immediately before it was banned (e.g., perhaps to index agreeableness when warnings about the ban were issued).

9 Discussion and Conclusion

In this study, we performed a large-scale computational analysis on Reddit conversations to understand when LSM occurs and its effect on platform engagement. Overall, do our findings indicate that LSM frequently occurs in online conversations within Reddit, and that it exhibits complex nonlinear relationships with conversation metrics such as Karma, conversation lengths, or controversy scores, which suggests linguistic influence can affect conversation dynamics. Furthermore, we show that the degree of accommodation in conversations is related to greater levels of engagement both at conversation and platform levels. Our findings highlight the possibility of identifying LSM as an indicator of engagement and civil conversations and suggest ideas for building and maintaining online communities that promote constructive discourse.

In our experiments, we have assumed LSM as a unidirectional concept by measuring the exhibition of a particular style conditioned on the previous turn. However, LSM can occur in several different directions, such as the two speakers converging into a single style or even diverging to separate styles. While not in the scope of this study, the existence of such types of LSM in Reddit conversation threads can be studies in future research.

10 Ethical Considerations

This study was conducted only on observational data and did not require any human intervention. We did not use any information that could identify individuals or specific demographic groups, and all of our presented results were obtained through aggregation from millions of users and comments.

Acknowledgments

This material is based in part upon work supported by the National Science Foundation under Grant No IIS-1850221.

References

Meghan J Babcock, Vivian P Ta, and William Ickes. 2014. Latent semantic similarity and language style matching in initial dyadic interactions. *Journal of Language and Social Psychology*, 33(1):78–88.

Jason Baumgartner, Savvas Zannettou, Brian Keegan, Megan Squire, and Jeremy Blackburn. 2020. The pushshift reddit dataset.

A Burcu Bayram and Vivian P Ta. 2019. Diplomatic chameleons: Language style matching and agreement in international diplomatic negotiations. *Negotiation and Conflict Management Research*, 12(1):23–40.

Biber. 1988. *Variation across Speech and writing. Cambridge : CUP*.

Eshwar Chandrasekharan, Umashanthi Pavalanathan, Anirudh Srinivasan, Adam Glynn, Jacob Eisenstein, and Eric Gilbert. 2017. You can't stay here: The efficacy of reddit's 2015 ban examined through hate speech. *Proceedings of the ACM on Human-Computer Interaction*, 1(CSCW):1–22.

Tanya L Chartrand and John A Bargh. 1999. The chameleon effect: The perception–behavior link and social interaction. *Journal of personality and social psychology*, 76(6):893.

Robert B Cialdini. 2001. The science of persuasion. *Scientific American*, 284(2):76–81.

Cristian Danescu-Niculescu-Mizil, Michael Gamon, and Susan Dumais. 2011. Mark my words! linguistic style accommodation in social media. In *Proceedings of the 20th international conference on World wide web*, pages 745–754.

Cristian Danescu-Niculescu-Mizil, Lillian Lee, Bo Pang, and Jon Kleinberg. 2012. Echoes of power: Language effects and power differences in social interaction. In *Proceedings of the 21st international conference on World Wide Web*, pages 699–708.

Cristian Danescu-Niculescu-Mizil, Robert West, Dan Jurafsky, Jure Leskovec, and Christopher Potts. 2013. No country for old members: User lifecycle and linguistic change in online communities. In *Proceedings of the 22nd International Conference on World Wide Web*, WWW '13, page 307–318, New York, NY, USA. Association for Computing Machinery.

Daria Dayter and Thomas C. Messerli. 2022. Persuasive language and features of formality on the r/changemyview subreddit. *Internet Pragmatics*, 5(1):165–195.

Erik W Doxtader. 1991. The entwinement of argument and rhetoric: A dialectical reading of habermas' theory of communicative action. *Argumentation and Advocacy*, 28(2):51–63.

Gabriel Doyle and Michael C Frank. 2016. Investigating the sources of linguistic alignment in conversation. In *Proceedings of the 54th Annual Meeting of the Association for Computational Linguistics (Volume 1: Long Papers)*, pages 526–536.

Howard Giles, Nikolas Coupland, and IUSTINE Coupland. 1991. 1. accommodation theory: Communication, context, and. *Contexts of accommodation: Developments in applied sociolinguistics*, 1.

Howard Giles, Tania Ogay, et al. 2007. Communication accommodation theory.

Amy L Gonzales, Jeffrey T Hancock, and James W Pennebaker. 2010. Language style matching as a predictor of social dynamics in small groups. *Communication Research*, 37(1):3–19.

Jack Grieve. 2023. Register variation explains stylometric authorship analysis. *Corpus Linguistics and Linguistic Theory*, 19(1):47–77.

Francis Heylighen and Jean-Marc Dewaele. 1999. Formality of language: definition, measurement and behavioral determinants.

Eduard Hovy. 1987. Generating natural language under pragmatic constraints. *Journal of Pragmatics*, 11(6):689–719.

Cornelia Ilie. 2021. Discussion, dispute or controversy? paradigms of conflict-driven parliamentary practices. *Journal of Language Aggression and Conflict*, 9(2):237–270.

Molly E. Ireland and Marlone D. Henderson. 2014. Language style matching, engagement, and impasse in negotiations. *Negotiation and Conflict Management Research*, 7(1):1–16.

Molly E Ireland and James W Pennebaker. 2010. Language style matching in writing: synchrony in essays, correspondence, and poetry. *Journal of personality and social psychology*, 99(3):549.

Molly E Ireland, Richard B Slatcher, Paul W Eastwick, Lauren E Scissors, Eli J Finkel, and James W Pennebaker. 2011. Language style matching predicts relationship initiation and stability. *Psychological science*, 22(1):39–44.

Elizabeth Jones, Cynthia Gallois, Victor Callan, and Michelle Barker. 1999. Strategies of accommodation: Development of a coding system for conversational interaction. *Journal of Language and Social Psychology*, 18(2):123–151.

Annemarie Kocab, Jayden Ziegler, and Jesse Snedeker. 2019. It takes a village: The role of community size in linguistic regularization. *Cognitive Psychology*, 114:101227.

Philipp Koncar, Simon Walk, and Denis Helic. 2021. Analysis and prediction of multilingual controversy on reddit. In *13th ACM Web Science Conference 2021*, pages 215–224.

Michael Lechner et al. 2011. The estimation of causal effects by difference-in-difference methods. *Foundations and Trends® in Econometrics*, 4(3):165–224.

Yinhan Liu, Myle Ott, Naman Goyal, Jingfei Du, Mandar Joshi, Danqi Chen, Omer Levy, Mike Lewis, Luke Zettlemoyer, and Veselin Stoyanov. 2019. Roberta: A robustly optimized bert pretraining approach. *arXiv preprint arXiv:1907.11692*.

Yelena Mejova, Amy X Zhang, Nicholas Diakopoulos, and Carlos Castillo. 2014. Controversy and sentiment in online news. *arXiv preprint arXiv:1409.8152*.

Antje S Meyer and Kathryn Bock. 1999. Representations and processes in the production of pronouns: Some perspectives from dutch. *Journal of Memory and Language*, 41(2):281–301.

Kate Muir, Adam Joinson, Rachel Cotterill, and Nigel Dewdney. 2016. Characterizing the linguistic chameleon: Personal and social correlates of linguistic style accommodation. *Human Communication Research*, 42(3):462–484.

Kate Muir, Adam Joinson, Rachel Cotterill, and Nigel Dewdney. 2017. Linguistic style accommodation shapes impression formation and rapport in computer-mediated communication. *Journal of Language and Social Psychology*, 36(5):525–548.

Sik Hung Ng and James J Bradac. 1993. *Power in language: Verbal communication and social influence.* Sage Publications, Inc.

Kate G Niederhoffer and James W Pennebaker. 2002. Linguistic style matching in social interaction. *Journal of Language and Social Psychology*, 21(4):337–360.

Bill Noble and Raquel Fernández. 2015. Centre stage: How social network position shapes linguistic coordination. In *Proceedings of the 6th workshop on cognitive modeling and computational linguistics*, pages 29–38.

Ellie Pavlick and Joel Tetreault. 2016. An empirical analysis of formality in online communication. *Transactions of the Association for Computational Linguistics*, 4:61–74.

James W Pennebaker and Cindy K Chung. 2007. Expressive writing, emotional upheavals, and health.

James W Pennebaker, Martha E Francis, and Roger J Booth. 2001. Linguistic inquiry and word count: Liwc 2001. *Mahway: Lawrence Erlbaum Associates*, 71(2001):2001.

Sudha Rao and Joel Tetreault. 2018. Dear sir or madam, may I introduce the GYAFC dataset: Corpus, benchmarks and metrics for formality style transfer. In *Proceedings of the 2018 Conference of the North American Chapter of the Association for Computational Linguistics: Human Language Technologies, Volume 1 (Long Papers)*, pages 129–140, New Orleans, Louisiana. Association for Computational Linguistics.

Daniel M Romero, Roderick I Swaab, Brian Uzzi, and Adam D Galinsky. 2015. Mimicry is presidential: Linguistic style matching in presidential debates and improved polling numbers. *Personality and Social Psychology Bulletin*, 41(10):1311–1319.

RL Street. 1991. Accommodation in medical consultations. *Contexts of accommodation: Developments in applied sociolinguistics*, pages 131–156.

Yla R Tausczik and James W Pennebaker. 2010. The psychological meaning of words: Liwc and computerized text analysis methods. *Journal of language and social psychology*, 29(1):24–54.

Paul J Taylor and Sally Thomas. 2008. Linguistic style matching and negotiation outcome. *Negotiation and conflict management research*, 1(3):263–281.

Michael Willemyns, Cynthia Gallois, Victor J Callan, and Jeffery Pittam. 1997. Accent accommodation in the job interview: Impact of interviewer accent and gender. *Journal of Language and Social Psychology*, 16(1):3–22.

Walt Wolfram. 1974. Sociolinguistic aspects of assimilation: Puerto rican english in new york city.

Yang Xu, Jeremy Cole, and David Reitter. 2018. Not that much power: Linguistic alignment is influenced more by low-level linguistic features rather than social power. In *Proceedings of the 56th Annual Meeting of the Association for Computational Linguistics (Volume 1: Long Papers)*, pages 601–610.

Author Index

Alkiek, Kenan, 64
Ananthasubramaniam, Aparna, 64
Anastasiou, Lucas, 39

Bose, Ritwik, 9

Caldwell, Matthew, 15
Chen, Hong, 64
Choi, Minje, 64
Clavel, Chloé, 50

De Libbo, Anna, 39
Dorr, Bonnie J, 9
Dunagan, Lavinia, 64

Fraser, Kathleen C., 25

Garí Soler, Aina, 50
Gong, Ziwei, 1
Griffin, Lewis, 15

Jurgens, David, 64

Kerkhof, Anna, 25
Kiritchenko, Svetlana, 25
Kleinberg, Bennett, 15

Labeau, Matthieu, 50
Litterer, Benjamin, 64

Mai, Kimberly, 15
Mavor-Parker, Augustine N., 15
Min, Qingkai, 1
Mozes, Maximilian, 15

Nejadgholi, Isar, 25

Pei, Jiaxin, 64
Perera, Ian, 9

Seth, Agrima, 64

Vau, Maria Do Mar De Almeida, 15

Yan, Jason, 64

Zhang, Yue, 1

Association for Computational Linguistics
209 N. Eighth Street
Stroudsburg, Pennsylvania 18360

ISBN 978-1-7138-8233-6

CURRAN ASSOCIATES INC.
proceedings
.com

4th Natural Logic Meets Machine Learning Workshop (NALOMA23)

Nancy, France
23 June 2023